THE LITERARY REVOLUTION

THE
LITERARY REVOLUTION

BY

STANTON A. COBLENTZ

*Author of "The Decline of Man," "The Thinker and Other
Poems," etc.; Compiler of "Modern American Lyrics"
and "Modern British Lyrics."*

NEW YORK
FRANK-MAURICE, INC.
1927

PRINTED IN THE UNITED STATES OF AMERICA
BY VAIL-BALLOU PRESS, INC., BINGHAMTON, N. Y.

TO
MY WIFE

CONTENTS

istics of the age; that he will define our time as one of flux, of motion, of fluidity, and of an instability verging upon chaos.

"The literary revolution of the early twentieth century," one can imagine him to write, "constituted the profoundest transformation since the Romantic Revival, but was more wide-reaching in its effects even than Romanticism, and for a while introduced an anarchy that played havoc with literary progress and productivity. It was not until after several decades that the confusion began to subside, the blatant-voiced and the hysterical died their natural death amid the tumult, the law-defying rebels became quiet respecters of law, and the way was made clear for that great company of fiction-writers and poets which appeared toward the middle of the century. . . ."

Even though the future critic should not be prompted to write in precisely these terms, it is at least probable that he will make some reference to our "literary revolution." In the dim and dwarfing perspective of time, that revolution may still seem as important in art as the Russian Revolution has been in politics, or it may dwindle to the dimensions of a Central American insurrection; but it does not require the detachment of a hundred years to convince one that a revolution has indeed been launched, that it gives evidence of being of tremendous magnitude and profound influence; that it partakes of the qualities of most rebellions in that it is nervous and disorganized, and that it is dominated by a reckless mob spirit, by virulent

CHAPTER I

INTRODUCTION

WHEN the literary historian of a hundred years hence pauses to survey our present poetry and prose, will he favor us with his approbation or dismiss us lightly with a mild disdain? Will he regard us with a respect as remote and formal as that which we accord to the unread Elizabethans? Or will he hold that our era is but the barren gap between Victorianism and the late twentieth century revival? Or, on the other hand, will he admit that the creative spirit was fruitful among us, but find its products as alien to his taste as the theology of a Milton or the pentameters of a Pope?

While of course the answer to these questions must be held by time, and by time alone, there are certain facts which we can foretell with definiteness as to the attitude of our twenty-first century successor. Whether he will regard our era as arid or fertile, contemptible or distinguished, it is fairly certain that he will find our epoch *different* from that which preceded it, and in all probability different from that which followed. Indeed, it is not unlikely that the changes now in progress will seem to him the prime character-

THE LITERARY REVOLUTION

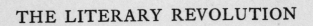

CHAPTER II

THE NATURE OF THE REVOLUTION

IT may seem a trifle misleading to give the name "revolution" to a multitude of remote and apparently disconnected influences. Yet most revolutions are incited by a number of parallel forces, aroused by the same causes and working toward the same end, rather than by one all-embracing and indivisible factor. While one may think, for example, of Danton or Robespierre as among the chief agents of the French Revolution, or of Kerensky, Lenin or Trotsky as leading figures of the Russian upheaval, yet one would not deny that the motivating power in both cases was a myriad of apparently unrelated deeds and external circumstances that stirred the minds of a myriad men simultaneously toward action.

And so it must be with revolutions in literature. Although apparently they sprout up as suddenly as mushrooms and represent the work of but a few individuals, their roots and feelers must reach far down into the hidden soil of literature and of life, and must draw nourishment from events seemingly as remote from them as the gropings of the earthworm from the bloom of the rose. Minor insurrections, to be sure, may be fanned artificially by small groups with de-

though he disagreed with me radically, for he might perceive that present-day literature is a chameleon that
varies in hue according to the observer and the point
of vantage; and in spite of his ready tolerance he might
be just a little amused, since—who can say?—the
names and the movements that appear mountainous to
us now might be invisible through the lenses of a hundred years, while influences and personages of which we
know nothing might shine as fixed stars.

And so, while realizing that the literary world in
which we live may have faded from the sight of later
observers, I shall endeavor to delineate the changes
which have transformed that world. I shall begin by
describing the nature of the literary revolution; next I
shall seek to depict its causes, in so far as they are dis-
cernible; then I shall devote several chapters to the
various effects of the revolution, to its influence upon
substance, form and ideals; and finally, having characterized the present tendencies and drawn my general
conclusions, I shall attempt to turn a speculative light
into the fog, and to catch fleeting glimpses of the unknown port toward which we are drifting.

work the peculiar hue of my own emotions, although I shall strive to avoid the distortion of my prejudices, and I crave pardon in advance if I am not successful in the latter attempt.   But I shall take an attitude which, I am well aware, will meet with no favor in certain influential quarters.   For the revolutionary tendencies in modern literature, which have been so highly and so widely applauded, have impressed me as mildly beneficial but primarily ruinous in their effects; and I have watched with growing disquietude as the rebels have won engagement after rapid engagement, and have captured citadel after citadel wherein Art once sat enthroned.

Candidly speaking, it seems to me that the cause of literature has suffered heavy losses, and is menaced, on the one hand, by indifference, stupidity and sheer dishonesty, and, on the other, by something numbing and leaden in the very spirit of the age.   And so ominous have been the recent transformations, and so triumphant the forces of destruction, that I can no longer keep silent the conviction which has been taking increasing hold of me during the past few years.

If I be in error in my central contention, I do not plead the right of a contemporary to make snap judgments or random guesses: however mistaken my conclusions may be, they are not hasty or ill-considered, but are the fruit of an outlook which I can no more avoid than I can avoid the appearance of the heavens to my open eyes.   Could our hypothetical future critic be with us now, he would pardon me, I know, even antagonisms and the tolerance of the torture-chamber, by a savage impatience with the existing order and an almost pathological craving to destroy.

Unfortunately, it is impossible for any contemporary to regard that revolution with the serene and unbiased eye of the future observer. Yet it is important that we not only realize that a revolution has been and still is in progress, but that we seek to discover its causes, analyze its nature, and weigh its effects. To accomplish any of these objects without prejudice would perhaps be beyond human power; the color of one's own views, the complexion of one's own emotions and imaginings, would inevitably tinge the result; and to do full justice to all one's contemporaries one would have to be that paradox—the perfect man. But any sincere discussion is preferable to none at all; and if one sets out with a recognition of the frequent temptations to error and of the inevitable limitations of all individual views and standards, it will perhaps not be amiss to describe and comment upon the literary revolution even without the advantages of historical remoteness.

Partly for this reason, but largely because I believe that the atmosphere needs clarification and certain enduring landmarks need to be pointed out, I shall attempt to devote the following pages to outlining and characterizing the literary metamorphoses of the last decade or two. I shall, of course, be actuated throughout by a point of view, which I am far from expecting every reader to endorse; I shall no doubt impart to the

liberate intent; but, unless they have some more fundamental cause, they are almost certain to be short-lived
as they are unnatural; and when a revolution extends
over a period of years, and goes thudding and rever-
berating to half a dozen diverse fields of art, one may
trace its sources to deeper ground than any mere artifice
or whim.

In the case of the literary revolution, one will find
not only that the origins are far down in the social
structure, but that the manifestations are so many and
so dissimilar as scarcely to be recognizable as phases
of the same phenomenon.   Expressionism in the drama,
imagism and formlessness in poetry, impressionism and
a chaotic diffuseness in the novel—these are but a few
of the products of the modern spirit, in so far as that
spirit is concerned with structure; while the peculiari-
ties of substance are so many as to require separate
enumeration.   But before describing those peculiari-
ties or dwelling upon the current singularities of form,
it will perhaps not be out of place to remark that the
seeds must have been abundantly sown before the
flowering plant could appear, so that we would have
had impressionistic plays even without our Georg
Kaisers and Elmer Rices, *vers libre* poems without our
Carl Sandburgs and Amy Lowells, and modernistic
fiction without our Ben Hechts and our Ethel M.
Kellys.

What, then, is the nature of that transformation
which is responsible for the new school of writers?   To
every person who has been so fortunate—or so un-

fortunate—as to read current literature extensively, an answer will at once be apparent; but it is doubtful whether the solution would in many cases be the same, for modern tendencies are to be seen in countless ramifications like the branches of a great tree. Yet a few basic facts will be agreed upon by all. To mention the most general first, there has been a change in spirit, a change as hard to define and yet as unmistakable as the difference in atmosphere between a Colonial mansion and a modern New York apartment. It is not precisely that the new literature is colder in tone or warmer than the old, or that it is more vividly lighted or dimmer; it is that the interior arrangements are not the same, that the walls and window spacings are not what we have been accustomed to expect, and that the whole is new and still reeks of putty and plaster.

The most obvious manifestation of the new spirit— and a manifestation that has wider implications than will at first be apparent—is its emphasis upon the hard-and-fast, the concrete, and the material. As opposed to the romanticism of a previous age, which delighted in a wide-ranging imagination and did not seek to sterilize its emotions with a dry reason, the modern writer insists upon an art that shall be based upon the tangible and the apparent; he makes a god of visibility, and prefers an easily seen skyscraper to all the vague castles of Camelot, the smoke of factory chimneys to the fogs of a fanciful Elysium, and beetles and house-flies to the ethereal and legendary skylark. For him there are no dim, remote sky-lines beyond which golden

wonders brood; there are no will-o'-the-wisps, no elfin
flickers or rainbow gleams, no fabled isles of the Hes-
perides; there are only stone pavements and brick
apartment houses, electric lights and motor cars, rail-
ways and bank accounts.   Truly, he is a superior creature to the child who lets his fancy create a fairy out of
a flower's face, to the savage who hears unseen phantoms rustling in the wind and rain,—truly, he is the
culminating product of the evolution of the ages, for is
he not as practical in literature as his friend the stock
broker is in finance?

As the inevitable outcome of this interest in the
visible and the material, modern literature tends to
exalt those ancient idols, the Superficial and the External; it aims to interest us almost wholly in things as
our senses represent them and, therefore, to make us
bow down at the altar of Surface Values.

Surface Values, indeed, have been sanctified and almost deified by the modern tendencies in spite of all
our confused strivings after profundity; and at the
same time (though there is a pronounced school of what
may be called the Obscurists) present-day literature
places much of its emphasis on things that are easy to
understand—easy to understand for the reason that
they are familiar and require no mental or imaginative
effort to be apprehended, but can be seen, heard or
felt, and (in many cases) smelt and tasted.

The worship of Visibility, of Surface Values, and of
Things Easy to Understand, is so widespread throughout our literature that examples will immediately oc-

cur to every reader. Half of the realistic novels of the day—and in particular those that ostensibly have a serious object—might be cited as illustrations in point; and at least half of the more widely applauded American poetry would furnish proof of our contention. Carl Sandburg's celebrated "Hog butcher for the world" is a perfect instance of the literary materialism that has been gaining increasing influence of late years; and other cases might be mentioned almost *ad infinitum*.

But a few typical specimens will suffice to make our meaning plain. Here are the opening lines of another poem by Mr. Sandburg:

> This bug carries spots on his back.
> Last summer he carried these spots.
> Now it is spring and he is back here again
> With a domino design over his wings.
> All winter he has been in a bedroom,
> In a hole, in a hammock, hung up, stuck away . . .

Certainly, this fulfills all the requirements of the school of Visibility, Surface Values, and Things Easy to Understand!

Or, again, consider the beginning of a typical sonnet by John Crowe Ransom—a sonnet typical not only of Mr. Ransom but of a whole school of writers:

> Paul, pinked with dozing, stood from the chair wherein
> Digestion was assisted after lunch—
> Roast chine and gravies, pudding, swigs of punch,
> His manhood being strong and it no sin
> To feed. . . .

Or, to take a final illustration, here is the opening of Louis Untermeyer's "Portrait of a Machine":

What nudity is beautiful as this
Obedient monster purring at its toil;
These naked iron muscles dripping oil
And the sure-fingered rods that never miss . . .

Hand in hand with the cult of the Material and the Superficial, there goes quite naturally the creed of the Rational. In eras of fettered imagination and restrained emotion, the human mind has always been wont to turn to a more or less mythical reason for guidance, and to make of *reason* a religion which it might superstitiously embrace. This was true in ancient Rome during the centuries of artistic barrenness; it was true in England during the eighteenth century, when prose was vigorous and poetry was drained of its essential nourishment; and it is not less strikingly true of the present era. Having shown our contempt for the old divinities—imagination and an unaffected emotion—we must necessarily find new divinities, since the mind must always have some pinnacle whereto to cling; and reason is the one obvious and the one possible substitute, not only because it is encouraged by the scientific atmosphere of the age, but because it is the logical reverse of those qualities which we have consciously discarded. How the use of reason has been abused, and how a false rationalism has hampered literary creation, will form one of the topics of subsequent chapters; but for the present, in listing the features of the literary

revolution, it will be sufficient merely to indicate the part that *reason* has played.

One of the natural parallels of recent rationalizing tendencies has been the gradual submergence of the beautiful. It is primarily in times of full-blown romanticism that literary beauty thrives (or, at least, that beauty which is of spirit rather than of form); and just as the eighteenth century in England was as remarkable for its scarcity of beautiful writing as it was notable for its dry critical atmosphere, so the present period has been witnessing an esthetic decline as marked as the growth of rationalism. The poetic quotations made above would alone suffice to give evidence of this development; but it is not by the testimony of any single work or group of works, but by the consistent perusal of scores, that one arrives gradually at the conclusion that beauty is one of the literary commodities no longer in demand. The hideous has been elevated to the plane of the magnificent, the puny to the plane of the divine; drain-pipes and bathtubs have been exalted to the status of nightingales and Grecian urns, and the typhoid bacillus has an equal ranking with birds of Paradise. Whereas the old bards would tell us

> Of something far more deeply interfused
> Whose dwelling is the light of setting suns

or remind us that

> Life, like a dome of many-colored glass,
> Stains the white radiance of Eternity,

the more recent poets prefer to discourse upon mush-rooms, cobblestones or sawdust, or to describe, as Stephen Vincent Benét has done,

> . . . the stuffy upholstered smell of the chairs . . .

or

> the blunt snouts of a dozen worms or so . . .

or to tell us that

> The member with the face like a pale ham
> Settles his stomachs in the leather chair.

In prose, as well, this tendency away from beautiful expression has been pronounced. How few, for example, are the W. H. Hudsons, who write of the dream-like magnificence of glimmering remote jungles, or glide forward to "A Crystal Age" of arcadian harmony and peace!—who catch all the faint trembling shades and gradations of loveliness, or who, in describing their heroines, would be so out-of-date as to mention "a hue in the half-hidden iris, brilliant and moist with the eye's moisture, deep with the soul's depth, glorified by the outward look of a bright, beautiful soul." Far more numerous and far more popular are the H. C. Witwers, who write full-length novels in the vernacular in some such fashion as this:

> "Honest to Dawes, any one who likes the wronger sex any better than I do shouldn't be allowed at large, no fooling! But I can take my boys or leave 'em alone, if you know what I mean. However, to get back to perfection in men—well, you might as well look for Ethiopian mayors in Georgia! There's a catch to the best of 'em. . . ."

After such a quotation, it would be superfluous to point out that good taste is not one of the accomplishments of the more modern writers. Indeed, it would almost appear that good taste is deliberately scorned along with all the finer graces; and there seems to be a singular conviction that a writer cannot be delicate and at the same time be robust. Comparisons may be misleading, but one is reminded of the small boy who displays a huge contempt for poetry and music because of his belief that they are meant only for girls, and so do not harmonize with his masculinity.

The natural outcome of this point of view is the worship of things of great physical strength and size. Just as our ten-year-old enthusiast may regard the pitcher for the local baseball team as the greatest man in the world, or may look upon the Woolworth Tower as in more ways than one the highest product of human genius, so the modern writer seems to be overawed by the presence of that which is large before the eye and fruitful in visible energy. Daffodils may have been a fertile subject for a Wordsworth, and daisies and field-mice for a Burns, but steel rails and iron girders are far more in accord with the modern spirit; and fictionists and poets alike (in America, if not in Great Britain) are so overwhelmed by the sheer mechanics of the age that they would scorn to write of the meadow grass and the lily when they might be celebrating the glories of furnace and steam shovel.

This is not true of all, of course, but it is true of an

excessively large percentage; so that while one will come across dozens of contemporary novels which exalt, let us say, the size, the wonder and the majesty of New York City, one will find comparatively few (except for the standardized western "thrillers") which depict the splendor and exaltation of the wide open spaces; and while one will hear abundant applause for the careers of those who accumulate much gold and so control the giants of Production and Distribution, one will read relatively little in favor of their obscurer relatives whose influence cannot be counted in stocks or bonds nor in town lots nor in country estates, but whose power is along the secret lanes and byways of the mind.

There is little consistency, however, even in this veneration of undisciplined brute strength; and it is a curious paradox that while, on the one hand, the new movement is largely concerned with the external and the artificial, on the other hand it is devoted to what it conceives to be the internal and the psychological. But in psychology, as in other fields, the revolution has penetrated the unexplored, has swept into virgin territory with triumphant flags; a new conception of the human personality has been conceived; and the High Priest of the modern cult is one Sigmund Freud, and the prayers of its votaries are offered at the altar of Sex. In later chapters we shall deal at greater length with this, as with other phases of the Literary Reformation; but it may be well, in passing, to point out that

the converts to the new creed are innumerable, and that they include such well known writers as D. H. Lawrence, Sherwood Anderson, W. L. George, Edgar Lee Masters, May Sinclair, and a host of others.

But even aside from the contributions of Freud and his disciples, a wave of eroticism seems to have swept through our literature to an extent that would have appalled our predecessors. The Victorians would not unnaturally have been bewildered and shocked; even the outspoken Elizabethans might have been a little sickened, for sex to them was something to be taken as a matter of course, and few if any of their number devoted themselves to its grosser and more morbid manifestations with the whole-hearted exclusiveness of the moderns. Open any contemporary novel by a writer celebrated or obscure, and one will have a fair chance of finding a "study" of sex in some of its more unsavory aspects; one may read a book-long account of a young girl whose chief claim to recognition is her scorn of the marriage ceremony, or of a young man whom some "suppressed desire" calls from his bride to his mistress upon his wedding day, or of a "sex-maddened beast" (I quote from a novel now before me) who consumes several pages in the act of triumphing over virgin innocence.

The reader will of course point out that our fictionists, in their preoccupation with sex, are merely building upon Continental models; but I would reply that they have gone far beyond Continental models, and that in a Flaubert or a Gautier or a Schnitzler there is a certain

sensitiveness and restraint which modern American and British writers appear to lack. Be that as it may, I shall later try to indicate that the current sex mania in literature is due less to individual causes than to something inherent in the spirit of the age; and at the same time I shall undertake to show that the nervous haste of much contemporary writing, its oddities and its eccentricities that at times verge upon madness, are likewise profoundly rooted in modern life.

As the natural corollary to the recent extension of literary subject matter to regions previously veiled, there has been a growing intimacy and informality of style, an informality which not infrequently brings one down to the colloquial level of undistinguished conversation, and on occasions (as in the above-quoted excerpt from H. C. Witwer) revels in a mud-bath of slang. This tendency has been almost equally in evidence in poetry and in prose, and every reader of contemporary literature will at once recall numerous examples; but in order to make my meaning clear beyond dispute, it may be well to offer several illustrations.

To begin with, consider the following, the opening of a story, "I'm a Fool," by Sherwood Anderson:

"It was a hard jolt for me, one of the bitterest I ever had to face. And it all came about through my own foolishness too. Even now, sometimes, when I think of it, I want to cry or swear or kick myself. Perhaps, even now, after all this time, there will be a kind of satisfaction in making myself look cheap by telling of it."

This is precisely in the modern conversational style; but not less in the approved current vein is the ending of the same story:

"And if I'm not another you just go find me one and I'll quit working and be a bum and give him my job. I don't care nothing for working and earning money and saving it for no such boob as myself."

Examples of these same informal and ungrammatical tendencies are singularly abundant in modern poetry— or what passes for modern poetry. Here, for instance, is the beginning of a piece by John V. A. Weaver, one of the most widely applauded exponents of the art of unstrained and natural verse:

> Say—listen—
> If you could only take a bath in moonlight!
>
> Hey! Can't you just see yourself
> Take a runnin' dive
> Inta a pool o' growin' blue,
> Feel it glidin' over you
> All aroun' and inta you.
>
> Grab a star—huh?—
> Use it for soap. . . .

In all the above cases the notable consideration is the spirit rather than the form of the work; yet form (or, rather, expression) has obviously received some attention, if only in the absence of polish.

As opposed to the above, however, there are whole broad classes of work in which form, while always in-

extricably interlinked with spirit, has the place of first
importance. And here, as so often in a survey of
modern literature, one comes across a striking paradox.
On the one hand, the interest in form manifests itself
in sheer formlessness, and, on the other hand, more
faithful to its ideal, it creates a sort of hollow container
from which all substance is excluded. Both manifestations of the preoccupation with form are fairly abundant, the latter occurring when there is a sort of fumbling return to the classical precept, the former when
the literary rebel abandons the old forms in favor of
chaos. It is chiefly in poetry that one finds that attitude which makes form parasitic upon substance; and
the offenders are not so much those traditionalists
whose lyrics are vacuous and fluent and whose sonnets
grandiloquent and uninspired, as those bolder spirits
who have dared to trample upon inherited ideas and to
wave the banners of what they call the "new rhythms."

Take, for example, H. D., whose work is commended
in H. P. Collins' *Modern Poetry* as "of definite significance to English literature." The following is the
beginning of what Mr. Collins terms her "most characteristic" poem:

> What are the islands to me,
> what is Greece,
> what is Rhodes, Samos, Chios,
> what is Paros facing west,
> what is Crete?
>
> What is Samothrace
> rising like a ship,

what is Imbros rending the storm-waves
with its breast? . . .

What is Greece—
Sparta, rising like a rock,
Thebes, Athens,
what is Corinth? . . .

What are the islands to me
If you are lost . . .

And so the author continues for dozens of lines. No
doubt she has given some attention to form, if only to
the extent of abandoning the old conventions—but who
can say that her work is not tenuous as sea-spray cast
up between the waves and the rocks?—who can
say that her verse is more than a net to catch the
mist?

In this case both major defects of the modern for-
malist—the lack of a significant subject matter, and the
want of a form that is not filmy and volatile—are sufficiently in evidence. But even in many instances
where the subject matter is vital, the author succeeds
in frustrating his own purpose by his neglect of form.
Thus, in scores of contemporary novels, one will find
a desultory quality and a diffuseness that would make
even "Nicholas Nickleby" or "The Old Curiosity
Shop" seem organic and unified by comparison. The
two most recent examples that occur to me are Sir
Harry Johnston's "Relations," which consist of little
more than a series of miscellaneous anecdotes mal-
adroitly patched together; and John Masefield's

"Odtaa," a work almost as disturbing as its title, since (despite some splendid passages) it begins like a text-book on geography, continues for many pages like a historical disquisition, and ends with "Appendices and Notes" after the fashion of a scientific essay or a treatise on political economy.

But if such crudity be irritating and at times even disconcerting, it is less confusing than that misapplied impressionism which is so prominent a feature of much present-day writing.

In itself, impressionism is, of course, a legitimate artistic device; but it has peculiar dangers owing to its artificial character, and must be employed with exceeding care and skill or not at all.   And care and skill are precisely what few living impressionists seem to exercise.   Some who are too indolent to elaborate a theme, and some who are incompetent to do so, appear to find pleasure in confining themselves to a few flashlight impressions when detail is obviously what is required—and the result is an amateurish incompleteness, dullness, obscurity, and, in some cases, sheer absurdity.

Consider, for example, the following six paragraphs which complete a typical chapter in a novel by one of our younger writers:

> "Judith was waiting for him at the sign-post.
> "He didn't want to face Judith.
> "He didn't know how to find the sign-post.
> "He had forgotten his directions.
> "He didn't care.
> "He left the room."

It is difficult to say what this resembles most nearly
—a story by an eight-year-old, or a poem in *vers libre*.
But at all events it is characteristic—characteristic of
a tendency to slash away at the sinews of an idea until
only the bare bones are left, and then to exhibit the
resulting skeleton as literary achievement.

A very similar disposition is manifested by what is
called Imagism—or, in other words, by that branch of
the free verse movement presided over by John Gould
Fletcher, Amy Lowell, and others of the less traditional group.   The above quotation from H. D. would
serve as an example in point; but, lest that illustration
be not sufficient, let me cite a few lines from "Willow
Poem" by William Carlos Williams:

> It is a willow when summer is over,
> a willow by the river
> from which no leaf has fallen nor,
> bitten by the sun,
> turned orange or crimson.
> The leaves cling and grow paler,
> swing and grow paler
> over the swirling waters of the river
> as if loth to let go . . .

Even in the drama—leaving out of account such ex-
pressionistic plays as "From Morn to Midnight," the satirical "Beggars on Horseback" and that muddled bur-
lesque, "Processional"—the newer forms and conventions have been finding favor.   If we no longer express
ourselves in blank verse of Shakespearean picturesque-
ness and rhetoric, we can at least write in free verse

that accords with all the formulæ of the latest authorities.   Thus, Harry Lee has recently written a prize play about St. Francis of Assisi in a sparse and bloodless *vers libre;* and thus, likewise, Alfred Kreymborg has composed several short dramas so successfully in the new medium that more than one anthologist has seen fit to represent him.   The opening of his "Rocking Chairs," which I find in one of Frank Shay's collections, will give a fair idea of his work:

MRS. ALMS.   A woman should not
        have ideas until after
        she weds, when the law,
        stamping her moral,
        gives her the privilege—

MRS. BOYLE.   within, of course,
        the circumscribed boundary,
        hermetically sealed.

MRS. ALMS.   Her views being legal,
        sacrosanct and free
        from anarchic tendencies
        of an individual turn,
        are certain to partake
        of assertions no more

MRS. BOYLE.   dangerous to the welfare
        of surrounding society

MRS. ALMS.   than is involved
        in discussions of,
        let us say

MRS. BOYLE.   the price of corn and butter . . .

The modern essay, alone of literary forms, has not felt the influence of anarchy such as the above. And that is probably because the essay is not, strictly speaking, a literary form. It is subject to none of the laws of creative art; it seeks not to weave an illusion, but to embody an idea; its organic structure is established by logic and not by the emotions or a cunningly controlled imagination. If one has no characters or situation or background to present, but only a point of view and nothing beyond, one would obviously stultify one's self by resorting to the artifices which our poets, fictionists and dramatists apparently mistake for art. And so the contemporary essay—while far from as outstanding and vigorous as one might desire—has remained relatively uncorrupted; and in so far as it has changed, it has been in the direction of a greater informality, a greater frankness and egotism, and a brusque ax-and-hammer quality such as one finds in the works of H. L. Mencken.

Overlooking the field of biography—which cannot properly be included in the domain of creative literature, and is so vast as to constitute a separate universe —we have now enumerated most of the leading tendencies sponsored by the literary revolution. But we have by no means touched upon them all; it would be possible to dwell at length upon the pessimism of much present-day writing, upon its hollow cynicism, its air of futility and disillusion, its unabashed egocentric leanings. All these subjects, however, may

safely be relegated to subsequent chapters; we have already dealt sufficiently with recent innovations to make plain their general nature, and are now ready to discuss the causes of the revolution before proceeding to a detailed consideration of the effects.

CHAPTER III

THE CAUSES OF THE REVOLUTION

A LTHOUGH literature of a high order may sometimes thrive on sparse soil apart from any direct connection with the life of the age, yet it is doubtful if any great literary revolt was ever totally independent of contemporaneous events and social movements. It would indeed be possible to imagine a Poe singing his ethereal songs or a Coleridge writing of his phantom ships or his "caverns measureless to man" regardless of the economic or industrial tendencies of the times; but it would be difficult to conceive of a Dickens launching into his attacks on lawcourt, school and prison without some sociological justification, or to picture an Ibsen inaugurating a mordant dramatic realism without regard to the facts of his experience and observation. Accordingly, the student of Ibsen or of Dickens would be certain to scrutinize the social environment under which the novels or plays were produced, for the attendant conditions of life would explain the authors quite as much as the authors in their turn would explain those conditions.

And so it is with the present literary revolution. If we would understand its causes, we must begin with a

study not of its artistic products but of its social background; we must try to determine how deeply the roots are entangled in recent historical movements, in economic transformations and in political events, in scientific progress or retrogression, and in the general acceptance of an idealistic or materialistic philosophy. To proceed otherwise than with reference to these hidden sources would be like trying to trace the development of a man's character without taking into account his early training and habits of life.

But once the inquiry is undertaken, the results prove fruitful indeed. Certainly the impartial historian, surveying at random the records of today and yesterday, could point to no age in which literary rebellion would seem more probable even were it not known to exist. For the present era contains in abundance most of those factors which make for a loosening of old bonds—those factors which tend toward anarchy, confusion, hysteria, and unceasing reaction and revolt. Whether or not we are prone to realize the fact, we stand at the crossroads in the world's history; civilization hangs wavering in the balance—on the one hand, the path winds upward toward renewed achievement, and, on the other, drops precipitously to black chaos.

Even had the present generation witnessed no important phenomenon outside of the World War, it would still have been one of the flame-bright generations of all time; but that conflict—great as it was in magnitude and effect—appears to have been little more than a logical incident in a social transformation that has been

culminating for over a century. Its lurid colors and
ghastly tragedies have given it a singular appeal for the
imagination, but all about us we can see outcroppings
of the historical metamorphosis of which it was but a
phase; we can observe a growing economic inequality
stretching a gaunt hand over whole great cities, and
industrial tumults reaching like red phantoms above
wide countrysides; we can observe imperialism stalking
about the globe with the padded tread of a beast of
prey, and militarism unbaring and sharpening its claws;
we can watch science donning the wizard's robe, and
conjuring up for us ingenious toys and not less ingenious
weapons with which to blast one another to bits; and
at the same time we can feast our eyes upon that
painted and powdered offspring of science and the new
economic régime—a strutting and bloated materialism
perhaps without parallel except in the most decadent
days of old Rome.

And all these developments—developments which
would each be sufficient in itself to cap an historical
epoch—are coming to a climax in our own age. Economic and social unrest, industrial conflict, international
rivalry, scientific innovations of an unprecedented nature, and a transformation in the very tenor and spirit
of life—assuredly, here are forces which must go
shuddering to the remotest corners of the world, and
could no more leave literature unaffected than they
could bring back the empire of the Ptolemies.

At first sight, it would seem that they would have one
of two effects: either they would open the way for

epics of the modern age, epics far vaster in scale than any that dealt with old Greece or Troy, or else they would leave our writers blinded and bewildered, aimlessly fumbling for their way, smitten by a blow whose source they do not know and whose nature they cannot understand. And it is the latter result, unfortunately, that has marked the course of modern social developments.

And so we find a curious confusion among those authors most affected by the troubled currents of contemporary life. Lacking perspective, they cannot see how they are caught in the web of extraneous events; they can view only the random manifestations of those events, while the great motivating causes lurk like unobserved shadows in the background; they are led to mistake the particular for the general and the part for the whole, like an ant that chances upon a human foot and believes it to be a mountain, eternal and self-complete. Hence their lot is really the pitiable one of the deluded groper. A dust-mote blown by the cyclone's breath is not more helpless than they; they apprehend only dimly that they are part of the swirl of cosmic and elemental forces; and, in their reeling confusion, they turn for understanding to their fellow dust-motes driven by the same universal storm. But no understanding is forthcoming, and they endeavor to explain all existence by reference to that which they chance to perceive—perhaps only some incidental little twist or eddy of the tempest.

To take a simple illustration, many modern writers

are obsessed with a vague distrust of life and a vague dissatisfaction; they realize that somehow something is wrong either with their lot or with the state of the world, and yet they could not tell one definitely what is awry; and their attitude toward the universe is one of half-suppressed hostility, which they may show in any one of scores of ways—by holding in general that life is all vanity and illusion; or by painting a series of promising careers that topple ignominiously into the mire; or by making their works chaotic in substance and idea, and transfusing them with a dark sense of struggle and frustration; or by attacking some particular institution which they may hold responsible for their discontent—the marriage system, or the Volstead Act, or any one of a thousand agencies great or small.

It is a peculiarity of human psychology that injuries not definitely understood may be ascribed to the remotest and most impossible of causes, and, through a process of association, may cause resentment to be transferred to an innocent object. Thus, if my friend John has wounded my sensibilities by criticizing my literary taste and I realize only vaguely the cause of my hurt feelings or can find no legitimate excuse for protesting, I may strike out in self-defense by diverting my anger to some apparently disconnected target, and may chide John upon his laxity in keeping appointments, or upon the carelessness of his attire, or upon his neglect of his wife.

And, in precisely the same way, if I be a writer and find myself out of accord with the currents of the times,

I may blame not the currents of the times but life itself
or any particular phase of life.   I may accuse the steam
railroads or the motor car of disturbing the pristine
peace and leisure of existence, when what I really abhor
is the industrialism of which the motor car is but a
product; or I may paint loathsome pictures of corruption and depravity in the great cities, when all the
while I feel no actual resentment at such corruption or
depravity, but am suffering because urban life deprives
me of proximity to those hills and fields I love.

And these are in no way extreme cases; if anything,
they are stated more mildly than the facts warrant.
There can be little doubt but that if we were to probe
to the roots of the pessimism, cynicism and despair that
feature so prominently in modern literature, we would
find in many cases that the causes were not what they
appear to be, but are grounded less in a specific discontent than in a wide maladjustment between the individual and the key-forces of the age.

Much more obvious are the sources of the literary
revolution when we consider the specific rather than
the general characteristics of the life of the times.
Perhaps the two most prominent features of the present age—at least, of the present age in the great cities
—are its overbearing materialism and its atmosphere
of nervous haste.   These, in their turn, are the products of industrialism and of the concentration of popu-
lation, and, when taken in connection with the two latter
factors, will furnish an index to most that is typical and
new in our life and our literature.

Let us consider, first of all, the materialism of our era, which is certainly its dominating force. Though it is to be doubted whether there was any period of history when materialism was not strongly entrenched —since men have always had certain animal needs to fulfill—it is also questionable whether many epochs have rivaled our own in their unashamed worship of sheer physical wealth and power and in their exaltation of goods over ideas, machinery over men. We have entered, without realizing it, upon a new era of the world's history; we have bowed down before rulers such as no past age has known, and our barons are our bankers, our kings our manfacturers and our great merchants; we have adopted a new religion, whose converts are numbered by scores of millions; and the visible symbol of that new religion is the silver dollar, and its rites are performed by the jingling priests of the Stock Exchange. And, not content with adopting the new creed, we have proceeded to canonize its most eminent practitioners, and the reverence which in past ages was reserved for the saints of the Church is now poured out to those more influential saints whose miracles are performed with gold.

But this is far from all. We have taken care not to make the new code too practical, but have fortified it with that mysticism proper to all religions; we have offered up our prayers at the altar of Unlimited Riches —a thing no one has ever seen, heard or felt; we have deified an abstraction, which we speak of respectfully as Millions of Dollars, and for the sake of that theoreti-

cal entity we are willing to sacrifice our labors, our comfort, our affections, even our lives. And so we lead existences that are well rounded, although well rounded in an altogether novel way, for whereas, on the one hand, we have a veneration for such concrete things as apartment walls, factory wheels and bank-books, yet, on the other hand, we are devoted worshipers of that invisible and intangible something which goes by the name of Wealth.

Since the new religion is so widely popular, it is inevitable that it should find many representatives among the writers of the day. And those representatives, following the established tenets of their cult, must give high importance to all physical articles, and particularly to such as can be the objects of barter; and at the same time they are expected to venture off occasionally into immaterial realms, although not into the old hackneyed domains of mounting aspirations and soaring souls, but rather into that higher empyrean where the great god Millions of Dollars rules the world from his lonely and unattainable throne.

As a result, we may observe those tendencies noted in the previous chapter—the worship of Visibility, of Surface Values, and of Things Easy to Understand. For, of course, while the god of the new religion is as unseen and unseeable as all true gods must be, the benefits he bestows upon his followers are not only quite visible, but are valuable chiefly upon the surface and, therefore, are easy to understand. Moreover, those benefits are of such a nature as to preclude the belief

that the universe can offer advantages of any other
kind; and once a convert of the new creed is convinced,
let us say, of the supreme virtues of fur coats or dia-
mond brooches or private yachts, it would be futile to
urge that there could be superior values in such unpur-
chasable commodities as nightingale songs or autumn
landscapes.

The writer of the new school realizes this fact, subconsciously if not directly. He understands that he is
appealing to an audience whose tastes are not those of
former audiences, but who care only for material things
and for the immaterial monetary Deity; and he knows
that were he to write as did his predecessors, and were
he to go careering off to "many-towered Camelot" or
to "faery lands forlorn," he might very quickly find
himself without readers. At least, he might find himself without readers among those numerous congregations which gather about the shrines of Material Comfort and of Money. And, if he himself were a member
of one of those congregations, the loss might be greater
than his code of ethics would permit him to sustain.
Besides, if he did not provide the multitude with its
desired fare, there would be others certain to do so;
and, in consequence, we would have modern realism
just as we have at present; and the hard-and-fast, the
concrete and the material would still edge their bristling
and inevitable way into our poems, our novels and our
plays.

At the same time as our writers pay homage to the
divinities of the pocketbook, they do unconscious def-

erence to the haste, the bustle and the strain of the age.
This is only fitting, since the haste, bustle and strain
are the ceremonials without which the new religion
could not be practiced. They are, in a way, rites sacred
to the Money God, and are among the means by which
the worshipers prove their faithfulness and make their
sacrifices. "Thou shalt not lose your seconds!" is the
first commandment of the exacting deity, who carries to
a logical extreme that most fundamental of all truths,
"Time is money." And, far from holding with the old
proverb that "Haste is waste," it imposes the doctrine
of "Hurry for hurry's sake," and makes time-murdering
a capital offense. Hence we find that many modern
men of affairs are as efficient as cross-country racers
when it comes to saving the fraction of an instant;
hence, also, we observe that the present era exhibits
one of the most singular contradictions in history, for
whereas no previous age could boast so many time-
saving devices, no previous age seems ever to have been
chronically so short of time.

And few previous ages have pressed their business
men and their writers quite so near to the fever-point.
Judging from the carelessness of most contemporary
prose, one would imagine that only the exceptional
author had the leisure necessary for expressing his ideas
with grace and clarity. Our novelists and short story
writers seem to have gone the way of quantity pro-
ducers in general; the demands of multiple production
have reduced their spare moments to a negligible mini-
mum, and they have no more time for the finer esthetic

details of their craft than they have for rebutting the popular conception of their work, "Art for the sake of gold." That haste which dominates the banker, the butcher, and the traveling clothing salesman—to mention only a few typical representatives of modern civilization—seems to have infected the creators of literature as well. In art, as in industry, the machine methods have been coming quietly and insidiously into vogue, and the rapid literary product has been triumphing over the precise, the abundant over the rare, and the standardized over the individual.

But there are at least two or three other ways in which the modern writer has been swayed by the impetuous currents of his times. In the first place, to begin with the most obvious, he has been urged to portray the restlessness and the hurry of modern life. The whirling of wheels, the racing of motor cars, the pursuit of some elusive Good amid an atmosphere of screeching subways and blatant horns—all constitute his inevitable subject matter; and while at times he may be a little inchoate in expression, a little less than photographic in his representations and a little more than confused in interpretation, it is but natural that his work should reflect to some extent the mad whirling and flitting of the storm-driven multitudes.

But in a still more significant respect his output is affected by the furious haste and urgency of life. Although he himself may not realize it, he is driven to depict objective and external things not only because these form the direct material of his experience, but because his time is so completely absorbed with non-essentials that—aside from lacking the leisure to give his work completeness and polish—he has not even a spare moment to commune with himself. And it is from self-communion that the greatest literature takes its birth. Wordsworth treading in lonely ecstasy the solitudes of his native woods and hills; Shelley seated in the seclusion of a pine grove, panting "for the music which is divine"; Spinoza meditating like an anchorite in the still privacy of his humble abode—here we find the dreamers of great dreams and the thinkers of high thoughts in that atmosphere of detachment and quiet which supreme philosophy or supreme creation demands. Imagine Keats writing his "Ode to a Nightingale" to the accompaniment of the shrieking and snarling of a steam shovel!—Imagine Milton launching forth upon the organ music of a "Paradise Lost" while crushed against the wall of a subway express, or Dante finding need of a fanciful Inferno if he dwelt among the brick ravines of a modern city!—Imagine the "Midsummer Night's Dream" composed to the raucous beat of jazz, or Gray's "Elegy" written in the space between a luncheon engagement and an invitation to tea, with the poet's watch on the table beside his typewriter!

True, Gray or Milton or Shakespeare or Dante might have been able to produce literature of a sort—the literature of objective realities—even had they possessed no outlook wider than that of five-story canyons and enjoyed no tranquillity undisturbed by the grinding of wheels and the thudding of motors. But their sense and appreciation of the beautiful would inevitably have been overclouded by the perpetual dreariness of the urban scene; and, racing from street to street and from hour to hour in a continual mania of time-saving, they would unwittingly have closed the doors of their own deeper personalities; they would have choked and thwarted that miraculous subconscious self whence thoughts and fancies arise like a magic bloom and out of whose depths genius struggles fitfully for expression.

This does not mean that they would not have risen to preëminence among their fellows. But it would have been a preëminence of the moment only; they would have expressed merely the superficial facts about the life around them; they would have fallen, as our writers have done, into the veneration of the blustering and the crude, the veneration of things of great physical size and strength; and, like our writers, they would have lived and worked in disregard of much that has vitalized the greatest literature and much that is fundamental in the soul of man.

And, like our writers in still another respect, they would have been influenced unconsciously if not directly by the audience for which they had to write. The turning from the outdoors to the indoors, and from the beautiful to the sordid, would have been encouraged by the artificial lives of many of their readers; by the fact that many, city born and bred, could not react to descriptions of natural loveliness for the reason that they had no personal acquaintance with such loveliness, and could not be drawn into imaginative or meditative moods for the reason that their environment and training and a false educational code had persistently stifled their imaginations and their capacity for individual reflection. Moreover, the readers, like the author, would be living lives of such commotion and strain that their own opportunities for self-communion would be negligible, and they would not be willing or able to give to books that leisurely, exclusive and thoughtful attention which the better books demand.

But to return to our modern writer—and to the specific impress which his work takes from the haste and tumult of the age. In addition to depriving him of the leisure for artistic completeness and of the time for self-communion, modern life sometimes produces in him an actually pathological effect. Under the continual strain and movement of a complicated existence, his nervous system may be dangerously affected; it may be tangled, twisted, or pulled ridiculously awry; he may develop abnormal susceptibilities, or abnormal irritabilities, or strange and unnatural tastes; he may seek relief from his repressions in outbursts of wild extravagance, or refuge from his jaded feelings by reversion to the frenziedly exciting and the primitive, or an outlet for his obscure resentments in moods that seem to verge upon madness, or deliverance from sheer boredom by eccentricities that leave his more sober-minded fellows bewildered and aghast. And all these blind and dimly comprehended forces will have their influence

upon his literary creation.   On the one hand, the effects
will be manifest in that wave of eroticism and that preoccupation with sex which we have already noted; and,
on the other hand, the results will be seen in a subject
matter that is vapid or obscure, and in an extreme
loosening of the bonds of form, as to be observed in
impressionism, expressionism, and *vers libre.*

One cannot help feeling, for example, that when an
author writes as does Marianne Moore in the following
passage, she must be suffering from some nervous com-
plaint which reverses the usual scale of values, and
makes the normal appear abnormal, the sane insane:

AN OCTOPUS

Of ice.   Deceptively reserved and flat,
it lies "in grandeur and in mass"
beneath a sea of shifting snow dunes;
dots of cyclamen red and maroon in its clearly defined
    pseudopodia
made of glass that will bend—a much needed invention—
    comprising twenty-eight ice fields from fifty to five hundred
    feet thick,
of unimagined delicacy.
"Picking periwinkles from the cracks"
or killing prey with the concentric crushing rigor of the
    python,
it hovers "spider fashion
on its arms" misleading like lace. . . .

And one suspects that it could be only an extraordinary state of nerves and feelings, a state perhaps
peculiar to our own age out of all the ages of history,

which could make any man write as does the author of
a poem recently selected as prize winner by one of our
more sophisticated magazines:

Quiet and green was the grass of the field,
The sky was whole in brightness,
And O, a bird was flying, high, there in the sky,
So gently, so carelessly and fairly.
Here, once, Indians shouted in battle,
And moaned after it.
Here were cries, yells, night, and the moon over these men,
And the men making the yells and cries; it was
Hundreds of years ago, when monks were in Europe,
Monks in cool, black monasteries, thinking of God, studying
    Virgil;
Monks were in Europe, a land having an ocean, miles of
    water, between
It and this land, America, possessing Montana.
(New York, Vermont, New Mexico, America has too).
Indians, Indians went through Montana. . . .

Since the latter poem won a prize, and the former appeared in a literary periodical of some prominence, and
since both have achieved considerable applause and
been reprinted in anthologies, it would seem that the
poets themselves are not the only victims of jaded
minds and abnormal nervous conditions.

All the causes of the literary revolution which we
have thus far enumerated—the unrest of modern life,
the maladjustment between the individual and the age,
the materialism and the frenzied haste of existence—are
furthered by other influences which do not take root
directly in social or industrial conditions, but which may

be termed practical or *artificial,* since they are deliberately planned and stimulated.   And the foremost of
these artificial agencies is the concentration of power
in the hands of literary cliques and dictators, who rule
with the arrogance of a Cæsar or a Mussolini, establish-
ing the taste of their followers as rigorously as the
Parisian designers establish the taste in women's
clothes, and substituting their whims and desires for
those standards which the writers and thinkers of centuries have slowly and laboriously erected.   Regarding
these cliques I shall speak at greater length in the
chapter on "Practical Factors Aiding the Revolution";
but for the present it will suffice to note merely that
they exist, and that they provide opportunities which
those of extreme tastes pursue avidly, and without
which the eccentrics might have no more than a normal
opportunity to propagate their work.

It is certain, indeed, that many of the more freakish
manifestations of the literary revolution, and many of
its harsher and more bristling aspects, are due to the
existence and the methods of the cliques; to their skill
in advertising and their persistency in spreading propaganda; to their fanning of literary effort where there is
no literary impulse, and their ponderous striving to be
original and clever; to their scornful intolerance of all
dissenters, their strutting self-sufficiency, and their disdain of the past; and last—and certainly not least—to
the ruthless employment of all those weapons which the
commercialism of the age thrusts into their hands, and
to a zeal in self-seeking which at times verges dan-

gerously upon the unscrupulous. Whether they have added any new tendencies is highly doubtful; but that they have accentuated the more radical of existing tendencies is unquestionable; and that they have consistently been on the side of confusion and anarchy is a fact implied by their very charter of existence.

With the mention of these artificial agencies of revolt we complete our enumeration of the leading causes of the literary revolution, and so may now turn to the somewhat broader and more intricate question of the effects.

CHAPTER IV

MODERN REALISM

SOME of the principal results of the literary revolution will be apparent from the foregoing discussion, since one could hardly describe the causes and the nature of any phenomenon without revealing much as to its effects. Even had the reader opened this book with no knowledge whatever of modern literary tendencies, he should now have some general idea not only as to their character but as to their influence; he should understand that our prose and our poetry alike have gradually been growing more matter-of-fact and less subjective,—except in the domains of Freudianism; that the imaginative and the beautiful have been withdrawing in favor of the sordid and the externally real; that a new code of the rational has arisen, a new materialism, and a new conception of art; that various innovations both in form and in subject matter have been adopted, and that in some instances these innovations pass the border-line of eccentricity.

But while the reader might have a few such broad impressions as to the effects of the literary revolution, he would not—were he previously uninformed—be in a position to describe those effects in detail, or to comprehend their specific nature. For the revolution in

literature—like most great revolutions—does not confine itself to a few simple and easily defined phenomena; the results are spread out in a vast network,
with countless intricacies and ramifications, like the
tangled foliage of a jungle. Accordingly, to arrive at
any understanding of what the modern movement has
meant, we must be prepared to consider it in detail and
to give a careful scrutiny to each of its outstanding
effects.

And if we proceed in this spirit, we will discover that
some of the chief forces put into operation by the revolution have been moving in one well-marked direction—
the direction of the new realism. Under this heading
may be classified a wide variety of factors, many of
which we have already noted: the emphasis upon Visibility, upon Surface Values, and upon Things Easy to
Understand; the tendency away from the ethereal and
the fanciful; the pre-occupation with the morbid and
the revolting, and in particular with sex in its less romantic aspects. But it shall not be our prime purpose
in this chapter to show directly how modern realists
make use of their subject matter. Rather, it shall be
our object to inquire into the spirit of their work; to
analyze it, and to determine whether or not it is what
it appears or professes to be; to ascertain in what obscure and impalpable ways it is transforming literature, in what ways it is doing that which no realism
has done before, and to what extent its influence seems
likely to be beneficial and to what extent injurious.

To make a broad general division, we might say that

there are today two chief schools of realism: the Psychological, and the Literal. While the former has gained numerous disciples, it is the latter that is more widely popular and that is more likely to be represented in any novel one may seize at random. Indeed, it would be no exaggeration to say that probably half the novels now issuing from the press belong to the school of Literal Realism. And by Literal Realism I mean that realism which is concerned chiefly with Visibility and with Surface Values. If we would employ another term, we might call it Reportorial Realism; for not only does it take as its motto that easily understood concept, "Things are what they seem," but it is engaged chiefly in reporting that which it observes, or, rather, that which it observes in exteriors.

In the light of such realism, all objects in the world of sense are of equal interest. A brick is as worthy of mention as a mountain, an ash-can as a marble palace; in fact, an actual ash-can would be far more worthy of mention than a merely imaginary marble palace; and the writer would esteem it his duty, however unpleasant, to make careful record of every refuse place and dumping heap that chanced to intrude within his line of vision. But in this pursuit he would be thoroughly single-minded and sincere; he would tolerate no compromise in the quest of Literal Truth; he would call a spade a spade even though his less conscientious fellows were content to call it a rake or a shovel or else to call it nothing at all; and he would make it his special mission to find as many spades as he could and to

exhibit them all where they could be seen and known by the world.

The distinguishing feature of the Literal Realists is their keenness of eyesight. Their eyes, in truth, have little less sensitiveness than the photographic camera; they are able to spy out and perpetuate a host of minute facts that less acute observers might miss; they could detect the one shadow on a sunny day, and the one pin-blemish on an else flawless canvas. And this is only to be expected, since their first love is Detail, and their favorite method that of the microscope. Having a finer sense of values than the average, they can observe the significance of phenomena that many would deem merely trivial and boresome; they would not scorn to devote a page or more to showing precisely how the hero of a story smoked his cigarette, or how the heroine bound her hair or powdered her nose, or how two of the incidental characters discussed the philosophy of corned beef and cabbage or of patent leather shoes.

Numerous examples of such delicacy of perception will at once occur to every reader; but the one that I myself recall most vividly is to be found in Sinclair Lewis' *Babbitt*, the first hundred pages of which are devoted to little more than a recital of how the hero got up in the morning, how he shaved and had breakfast, how he went down town and conducted some questionable business deals, and how he returned home again in the evening.

But regarding *Babbitt* and the countless books of its

type, there must always be a wide difference of opinion. In the conception of the Literal Realists, such works represent high creativity, for they are scrupulously faithful to the details of observed fact. In my own estimation, they are not art, and do not even approach the boundaries of art, any more than the average newspaper reports approach those boundaries, though these reports at least have the merit of brevity. But they are lacking in precisely those qualities which all great literature —and all moderately good literature—must possess; they explain nothing, they interpret nothing, they vivify and animate nothing, they produce no illusion in the reader's mind, they fail to employ that selective faculty, that discipline and restraint which is the peculiar weapon of the creator.

There are, of course, many gradations of merit and accomplishment, and a few of the Literal Realists succeed where the multitude fail. Knut Hamson, for example, has employed the Literal method to good effect in his *Growth of the Soil*. But here the method is essentially in place, for the reason that the situations and characters are primitive and simple, their actions without complexity, and the whole atmosphere of the virgin woods so far from the normal civilized atmosphere as to make each detail a revelation and to give each bare fact and incident a significance which familiarity would have vitiated.

But the themes in which Literal Realism may be employed so effectively are comparatively few. Its gen-

eral tendency has been to clog the currents of literature
with inert and wooden material; to propagate the commonplace, to multiply the uninspired, and to accentuate
the petty and the dull. It has been, in a word, one of
the dreariest and deadliest of influences; it has injected
into literature something of the spirit of a prosy and
gossip-loving old aunt; it has been the foe of all that
is ecstatic and youthful, of the daring imagination, of
that romance which lies beyond the horizon and that
adventure which would bear one to undreamt-of stars.

Much the same may be said of the second school of
realism, which we have termed the Psychological. But
here the forces at work are vitally different: there is an
attempt at analysis, an attempt at profundity, an attempt at piercing beneath the armor of life. From
what we have already stated, a fair amount should be
apparent as to the general nature of this faction; it
should be evident that it is serious in its aims, but that,
like the Literal group, it has a creed and dogmas all
its own; that it is inclined to be cynical, skeptical, and
pessimistic, and that its entire conception of the human
personality is built about a single word—the word sex.

This term, however, has not the same meaning for
our Psychological Realist as for the writers of the past;
it is not some exalted essence whose proper name is
Romance and whose normal manifestation is Love; it
is not some mysterious emanation more of the spirit
than of the body, the occasion for lyric ardors and an
awe and a veneration as of one who stands with head

unbared before the shrine of a god. "Away with all
your silly sentimental theories!" cries the Psychological
Realist. "Too long our poets and romanticists have
been filling us with maudlin nonsense; now it is time
for the veils to be drawn and the truth to be told!"

Having begun with this bold declaration, our Psychological writer proceeds to draw the veil and to tell
the truth according to his own lights. And he succeeds far more thoroughly than one might have expected; he is as original as he is earnest—and how
vastly changed is the world after he has painted it!
Assuredly, here is a new illumination and a new understanding; we see that the Literal Realists were wrong
after all, and that things are not what they seem.
Contrary to all appearances, the human universe is
composed of a multitude of instinct-driven animals,
each governed by that dominant law, the impulse of
reproduction; and, under the influence of this sovereign
principle, they are committing absurd and even dis-
gusting actions whose nature they themselves do not
fully realize; they are conceiving all manner of illicit
attachments, suffering from all manner of damaging
suppressions, and forming ineradicable complexes which
threaten to warp and even to ruin their personalities.
Thus, mother and son or sister and brother or friend
and friend may be caught in a web of Sex that entangles
them as a spider entangles a fly; thus the human mind
may be the cage for a multitude of deeply hidden and
growling forces that may leap forth at any time and
shake it like an earthquake; and thus, also, we may

have a conception of human relationships that is utterly novel and that is as epoch-making as it is disturbing.

And upon that conception a whole library of new literature has been founded. Psycho-analysis and the Freudian theories in general have been accepted as established truth, regardless of the fact that there is disagreement even among psychologists; and with the key of a new knowledge, our writers have proceeded to unlock door after hidden door of the human personality. But it is precisely at this point that they lay themselves open to criticism. We must recognize, to begin with, that their work stands as a more or less natural reaction to the sentimentalism of a previous age, and that their unlimited frankness is the logical reverse of the reticence of the past. But we must also realize that, like so many other rebels, they have swung the pendulum with too much force and sent it rattling from extreme to extreme. Though they maintain that their views are both scientific and logical, they have in reality proved themselves to be most unscientific and most illogical; they have shown an uncritical faith by assuming the validity of hypotheses whose full force is yet to be demonstrated.

That there are large elements of truth in the doctrines of Freud seems to be the general consensus of opinion, and there is every reason for believing that time will endorse some of his conceptions. But just how great those elements of truth may be, and just which of the conceptions time will favor, are questions that even the trained psychologist would hesitate to answer with finality, and that would seem to be utterly beyond solution by the mere littérateur. Yet, with a boldness that one can only marvel at and admire, this is precisely where the littérateurs do offer their solutions. So utterly courageous are they that their usual procedure is to accept the new tenets in their entirety, as though there never had been, never would be and never could be any doubt as to their full authenticity.

And thereby, it seems to me, the writers of the new school are making a mistake that will perhaps prove fatal. A poem that builds up its magnificent music about a false creed (for example, *Paradise Lost*) may possibly endure despite its lack of foundation; but a novel based on an erroneous doctrine is almost certain to be swept at once into the dust-heap. And all our Psychological Realists are constructing their work on doctrines which, if not erroneous, are at least highly questionable, and which a later age may thrust aside like so much straw. The fact which they do not seem to recognize is that psychology is not as yet a developed science; that it has only recently awakened at all, and that we are apparently at the dawn rather than at the noonday of psychological investigation; that the human personality is still for the most part an unfathomed mystery, and that a few years hence we may reject the notions prevalent today, just as, in the domain of physics, we have discarded yesterday's belief in the conser-

vation of matter and the indivisibility of the atom.
And so our Psychological Realists are a little in danger
of impressing our successors somewhat as we are impressed by those old theorists who held that the sun
revolved about the earth or that a ship might topple
off one of the world's flat edges.

Although the Psychological and the Literal writers
are so widely at variance in aims and methods, yet in
their ultimate nature and in their influence they have
many points of similarity if not of identity. And this
is chiefly true with regard to their limitations. For
both schools have one fundamental shortcoming, which
is responsible for a multitude of lesser drawbacks, and
which of itself would be sufficient to vitiate much of
their work: they sponsor that realism which is not true
to reality. In other words, their particular variety of
realism is not in the broader sense realism at all, and
comes little closer to the ultimate truth than does the
work of the most extravagant romanticist. This is not
to say that they necessarily err in the reporting of fact,
either physical or psychological; it is not to imply that
they cannot tell us accurately how their characters be-
have in office, street or home, and cannot describe with
fidelity the atmosphere of a city or of a farm; but it is
to contend that their work lacks that completeness and
that balance without which no literature can fit the pattern of actual life.

And the reason for this may be very briefly expressed: the method of modern realism is one of half-

truths. Accurate as it may be in its observations and veracious with regard to detail, it fails to give a well rounded and comprehensive picture of life; in fact, it gives a picture that is decidedly distorted, and distorted less because of what it includes than of what it neglects to include.

Imagine, for example, a man who, upon observing the rainbow for the first time, would exclaim, "Ah, the rainbow is red!" And imagine how, seeking to substantiate his contention, such a man might point upward and call attention to the red bands in the celestial arch. Would any of us care to deny that the rainbow has red bands? And would any of us believe that sufficient excuse for calling the rainbow red? Why not call it green, or blue, or lavender, for does it not contain streaks of those colors as well? Of course, the truth would be that it is neither green nor blue nor lavender nor red—and a similar truth applies to life as well. The literary observer of the realistic school, looking up at life with puzzled scrutiny, observes a red coloration and promptly informs us that life is red; but the purple and yellow and orange and azure elude his gaze. And his defects of vision are not mitigated by the fact that writers of other schools may make similar mistakes; that the romantic may tell us that life is a cerulean blue, and no other tint or shade; or that the more imaginative writer may find it to be of the hue of pearls or emeralds or jade or alabaster.

But precisely which of the colors of life do our realists overlook? Before proceeding further, we may re-

mark that their omissions and oversights cannot be
listed under any single heading. In general, however,
their error is the great error of the inductive method:
the fallacy of reasoning from the particular to the universal. Like the scientist who finds the jaw-bone of
some long-extinct human and resurrects a vanished race,
the realist seizes upon some dried bone of observation
and builds for us a picture of life. The difference,
however, is that the scientist has such a mass of sub-
stantiating data to work from that the chance of error
is negligible, whereas the creative writer more often than
not has but a few facts,—facts necessarily of incon-
siderable extent by comparison with the volume of ascertainable knowledge. Thus, he may have experienced
a life of hardship, sorrow and disillusion, and so may
picture the world as a cheerless and barren place; or
he may have suffered repressions which have developed
a sex complex, and which induce him to write as though
all other men had twisted personalities; or he may
have observed several instances of marital disagreement, and so may express himself with the weary cynicism of one who knows that happy marriages are
impossible; or he may have encountered sundry cases
of crass self-seeking and corruption, and so may depict
the world as though common kindliness and consideration were to be expected only in Utopia.

For my own part—and here again I am speaking only
of a personal prejudice—I frequently have a most curious and unsatisfactory feeling when reading one of
these modern books that aim to show life, and to show

life naked. I have the impression that their peculiar brand of ugliness is no nearer to the heart of things than the remote beauty of *Kubla Khan* or *The Faerie Queene;* that their peculiar pessimism is as little reliable as the optimism of a Pollyanna; and that their creed of failure and despair is about as worthy of serious consideration as the success doctrine of Orison Swett Marden or of the "American Magazine."

But even though these particular impressions be utterly mistaken, there is no doubt in my mind that our realists on the whole disregard some of the larger aspects of reality. Whether they be concerned with showing the devious workings of some pathetic and mania-ridden psyche, or whether they aim merely to show how John and Mary set up house together, balanced the budget and trained the children, most of our modern realistic works are written with a sort of blindness to the unapparent, a mole-like burrowing which can take account of nothing outside the mole-track. After all, the record of actual life must be something beyond a catalogue of facts and numbers and events; it must tell us something more than that Mrs. Brown went to church on a certain Sunday, or that Tom met Ellen at a house party; and it must not try to complete itself even by informing us that the young lady wore a blue gown or that certain distorting influences were at work in Tom's mind or in Ellen's. If it deals at all with such exterior facts as names and streets and motor cars and houses, it must treat them as mere details in an intricate and organic whole whose name is Life; and it must recognize Life not merely as a thing to be witnessed, but as a thing to be felt and imagined.

For the vision that is essentially required is that which does not identify Reality with Material Reality. It cannot be emphasized too strongly that mere physical happenings are far from making up the totality of life; that each of us lives a whole existence in a world whose boundaries are unseen, whose adventures stir no vibration in the turgid universe of sense, and whose triumphs and direst sufferings are remote from our neighbors as happenings on the planet Mars. Fantastic imaginings and futile dreams, vehement hopes and brooding despairs, incredible longings and sorrow and exaltation and tenderness and fire—these are the things which make up reality, the things which make up life. They are also the things that no one will ever witness, no matter how long he be trained as an observer, and that, moreover, no one will ever divine by means of any scientific or psychological theory. For the great touchstone to these supreme facts is Imagination, and the password is "Beauty"; and it is precisely beauty and imagination that our present realists have most neglected.

So vital is the oversight in each case, and so fundamental its influence upon literary development, that we will require a separate chapter for the treatment of each of these subjects. But before turning to a discussion of literary beauty, we will consider that Decadence of the Imagination and that simultaneous Elevation of the Rational which are among the most striking tendencies supported by realists both of the Psychological and of the Literal schools.

CHAPTER V

THE DECADENCE OF THE IMAGINATION

> We are such stuff
> As dreams are made on.
> SHAKESPEARE, "The Tempest."

IF all the literature of the newer type were to be gathered into a great heap and boiled down in some enormous crucible, the residuum might be rich in certain ingredients such as candor, directness and detail, but it would also be deficient in more than one essential. And among the elements notable for their scarcity would be a creative imagination. Indeed, one might have to fumble about for some time before one found any trace at all of imagination, and then it might prove to be of so poor a quality that its true nature would not be apparent. It might not have its usual light and flexible character, but might be stiff and heavy with earthy adulterations; it might exhibit traces of the effort to water it to the point of impotence, or else might show signs that its very existence was accidental and that it had crept in unnoticed in spite of an effort to keep it out.

For the sad truth is that imagination has fallen into disfavor. "Ever let the Fancy roam" may have been a suitable theme for a Keats; but the modern would reply, out of the assurance of his new theories, "Keep the Fancy safe at home." It may be that he would not make such a reply consciously, for certain traditions are too overawing to be opposed in words however consistently they may be violated in action. But the fact remains that of late years there has been a growing distrust of imaginative things, a growing tendency to hitch literary expression to the lamppost rather than to the stars, and a dimly apprehended but definite movement to confine poetry and prose to the "safe and sane" —which means to those facts that a camera or a phonograph could record.

The modern writer, while still a little dazzled at the word "Imagination" and still claiming to worship the falling god, would keep that deity caged and confine its authority to the near and the familiar; he would make of Imagination a sort of domestic divinity, whose shrine is the hearthstone, the sofa or the door-mat, and whose temples, accordingly, could never be reared amid the snows of untraveled mountains or in the gloom of uncharted seas. "Let the data of your experience furnish the fuel of your fancy!" cries the modern sage, quite regardless of the fact that the data of experience must always furnish the fuel of fancy, but that the further fancy escapes from experience the more vigorous and the more authentic it becomes.

The modern method is to make fancy always bear a sooty empirical imprint; to keep it obvious and earthbound; to see that it imposes no strain upon the practical-minded and arouses no suspicion in those who believe that their five senses show them the whole of reality.   This is true both of the Literal and of the Psychological schools, for imagination would be as a lethal poison to the former, and might awaken damaging doubts in the latter.   Moreover, it might offer our writers the opportunity to regard themselves in proper perspective, and so might prove not less excruciating than a sense of humor.   But there is little present prospect that the modernists will suffer from such painful self-recognition.

For they are resolutely bent upon producing that sort of realism in which imagination is shoved into a minor rôle.   This is not to imply that realism and imagination are necessarily antagonistic; there have unquestionably been countless realistic works wherein a robust imagination has effectively functioned.   But in all such works the raw material of experience has been refined and altered, new situations and characters have been summoned forth, and a whole world has been created which does not correspond with the world of observed fact and yet actually exists for author and reader alike.   Thus, the works of Dickens, of Thackeray, of George Eliot, are all realistic in the sense that they do not venture far from observed fact.   Yet each of these authors has created a universe which his imagination has made subtly but essentially different from the external universe.   In the eccentricity of a Betsy Trotwood, the droll good nature of a Twaddles, the slightly ridiculous entanglements of a Pendennis, the suppressed fire and vehemence of a Maggie Tulliver, we are introduced to scenes and characters that are closely akin to the scenes and characters of the life we have witnessed, and yet somehow are distinctively different—and the difference is due to the transfusing power of imagination.

It is precisely this imagination that modern realists seek to avoid, in so far as they are able—though, fortunately, they are not always able. They aim less to create than to reproduce, and less to be interpretive than to be accurate. They take a sort of plaster cast of life, without consciously enlarging or suppressing any detail, and they present us the result with the confident label, ART. And whether that plaster cast is represented by a novel many hundred pages long, or by a sketch of a dozen lines, the work is almost certain to be vitiated by its imaginative sterility.

Consider, for example, the following excerpt from the *Spoon River Anthology*—a book whose general conception shows an imagination lacking in its component parts:

> I went to the dances at Chandlerville,
> And played snap-out at Winchester.
> One time we changed partners,
> Driving home in the moonlight of middle June,
> And then I found Davis.
> We were married and lived together for seventy years,
> Enjoying, working, raising the twelve children,
> Eight of whom we lost
> Ere I had reached the age of sixty.
> I wove, I spun, I kept the house, I nursed the sick . . .

Now let us examine by contrast a passage from an older and somewhat more celebrated poem:

> She dwelt among the untrodden ways
>   Beside the springs of Dove,
> A Maid whom there were none to praise
>   And very few to love:
>
> A violet by a mossy stone
>   Half hidden from the eye!
> Fair as a star, when only one
>   Is shining in the sky.

Regardless of the technical differences between the two works, is not the difference of atmosphere at once apparent? Is it not evident that Wordsworth was working under the transmuting influence of a strong imagination, whereas Mr. Masters employed no imagination whatever? The bald statement of the facts regarding dances, moonlit drives and the raising of children, with only the omission of a commonplace suggested incident, requires about as agile a fancy as is necessary for shoveling coal or running an adding machine; while only the creative artist would be likely to think of "a violet by a mossy stone" or of "a star, when only one is shining in the sky."

And such examples might be multiplied indefinitely. It will hardly be possible to offer any quotations from current novels or plays, since it would be necessary to reproduce whole acts or chapters; but another illustration from present-day verse will perhaps be in point. Here, for instance, is the beginning of Harriet Monroe's piece entitled "The Hotel"—which, incidentally, is typical of the method of Literal Realism:

The long resounding marble corridors, the shining parlors
    with shining women in them.
The French room, with its gilt and garlands under plump
    little tumbling painted Loves.
The Turkish room, with its jumble of many carpets and its
    stiffly squared un-Turkish chairs.
The English room, all heavy crimson and gold, with spread-
    ing palms lifted high in round green tubs.
The electric lights in twos and threes and hundreds, made
    into festoons and spirals and arabesques, a maze and magic
    of bright persistent radiance.
The people sitting in corners by twos and threes, and cooing
    together under the glare . . .

Perhaps it is only a matter of personal taste, but
somehow I cannot help preferring that other kind of
description which we find in Tennyson:

> There is a music here that softer falls
> Than petals from blown roses on the grass,
> Or night-dews on still waters between walls
> Of shadowy granite, in a gleaming pass;
> Music that gentlier on the spirit lies
> Than tired eyelids upon tired eyes . . .

And somehow, while Miss Monroe's piece leaves me
unaffected, I find my whole spirit lifted up and transformed when Arthur O'Shaughnessy sings of

> The splendid fearful herds that stray
>   By midnight, when tempestuous moons
> Light them to many a shadowy prey,
>   And earth beneath the thunder swoons

or when Shelley compares the moon to

> . . . a dying lady lean and pale,
> Who totters forth, wrapped in a gauzy veil,
> Out of her chamber, led by the insane
> And feeble wanderings of her fading brain.

Why is it that descriptions such as Miss Monroe's are powerless to entice and hold the reader, while a single phrase from Tennyson, O'Shaughnessy or Shelley is enough to bind one in a magic web?

Let us overlook for the moment the effect of the rhyme and meter in the older poems, and the captivating influence of their beauty of atmosphere; for while these elements are of fundamental importance, their power would probably be slight except for the aid of an all-suffusing imagination. Music softer than "petals from blown roses"; walls of "shadowy granite"; "fearful herds" that stray beneath "tempestuous moons"; the dying moon-lady "led by the insane and feeble wanderings of her fading brain"—these are the things of which literature is made, the things that draw the human soul toward them in ecstasy and wonder. Yet they are not the things that the writer has directly seen, heard or experienced; they have not the concrete and indubitable reality of "The French room, with its gilt and garlands" or "The Turkish room, with its jumble of many carpets"; they have been perceived not with the vision of the eye but with the vision of the imagination, that imagination which sees where careful observation is blind and that enters where reason will not dare to tread, so arriving by a process akin to intuition at truths which mere common sense could never have discovered.

For, paradoxical as it may seem, imagination is often the lantern that lights the way to a reality higher than the orthodox reality of ascertained fact. It is not only by means of the pick-ax and shovel that one can pierce to the heart of things; a single revealing flash of light may penetrate further in the millionth part of a second than the plodding metal can dig in days. And it is precisely such a light whose services the realist has eschewed in favor of tools of steel and wood. "Do not show us the way to the clouds!" he pleads, as though he could prove his superiority by keeping nearer to the earthworm; and, scorning that illumination which unbares the heavens above and the rocks and waters beneath, he goes plowing away with mole-like face unswervingly upon the ground. For he has none of that enthusiasm which uplifts and none of that insight which transcends all logic; he is like a sober and practical-minded middle-aged man, while his more imaginative fellow is a daring and enthusiastic youth. With the one goes all the caution, the disenchantment, the materialism of advancing years; to the other belongs the fire, the courage, the adventure of awakening manhood. And which will it be, the ardent youth or his staid and settled elder brother, who will blaze the new trails and chart the unexplored? Which will it be that will plunge and dare, that will aspire and soar, and that will clutch at new truths and uncover new experience? The realist has all the advantages of the tried and trodden paths, of security and of the matter-of-fact—but is it not the imaginative non-realist that will go voyaging forth with the recklessness and the determination of the young, and so will make discoveries and reveal the world in a fresh and clearer light?

In order to make our meaning plainer, a few illustrations may be in point. Thus, if the realist wishes to paint life as a good and a happy thing, he will show us a contented family or a contented community in modern New York or New Jersey; whereas the romanticist will picture two lovers strolling among the woods of Arcady, or else will summon forth an assemblage of serene spirits in an unmapped realm somewhere between the sunset and the stars. The first method will appeal to the reader who can conceive only of what he sees and experiences, whereas the second will be as the unfolding of magic doors to him who has eyes in his imagination. Or, again, the realist may wish to show the warping and ruinous effect of modern industry, and may do so by means of detailed accounts of the Massachusetts cotton mills and of the lives of particular workers; whereas the more imaginative writer, attacking the same theme, would create a country of his own, perhaps in the center of the earth or on Mars or the moon, and would illustrate by vivid analogy the nature and tendency of conditions as he observed them. His method would be a more difficult one, for he would have to build out of the thin stuff of fancy; but the results might prove worthy of the effort, since he would provide a detached point of vantage whence one might look at the world in a fresh light.

Many novels, of course, have indicated the evils of a mechanical civilization by picturing them in a realistic fashion—but how many have succeeded so well as has Samuel Butler's *Erewhon,* which portrays for us a land that never existed, and tells us how the people of that land that never existed destroyed all their machines lest the machines destroy them?   Somehow, although the idea is not altogether novel, it is presented in such a way as to strike the reader's mind irresistibly—one is bound to pause and to reflect upon the fact that the people of Erewhon have destroyed their machines; and, once one reflects, all the implications of the situation will be clear, and one's memory will be likely to retain a lasting impression.

But it will perhaps be contended that the example of *Erewhon* is not entirely in point, since the author has aimed to be satirical and thereby to present ideas, whereas most novels are not satirical and do not deliberately present ideas, but seek rather to cast illumination upon the obscure places of the human mind and character.   All very true—but if the more imaginative writing be best suited for the embodiment of ideas, that alone is a decided point in its favor.   If we desired, we might linger over this subject for pages, providing examples from some of the most thoughtful writers of the past and present, from Swift and Voltaire, from Bellamy and Mark Twain, from Lord Dunsany and

H. G. Wells, from Anatole France and Bernard Shaw.
But it will perhaps be more convincing to offer illustrations from one or two authors whose works are not designed primarily to inculcate a point of view.

Take, for instance, James Stephens' *The Crock of
Gold*, a humorous and imaginative novel which bears
us to an utterly fabulous Ireland of leprechauns and
gods and speaking beasts, and yet offers us many shrewd
and human and quite convincing insights into life and
character.   Or consider W. H. Hudson's *Green Man-
sions*, probably one of the finest romances of all time,
and yet one of the most fantastic books of its day.
Here, in a jungle-land whose precise location is never
revealed but whose details are admirably imagined by
the naturalist-author, we are introduced to the bird-
maiden Rima, a creature so exquisite and so ethereal
that she seems more like the incarnate spirit of the
flowers or the dew than like any mortal being.   Yet
this fairy-like girl, who would answer none of the tests
of reality imposed by any of our literalists or psycho-
analysts and who seems less akin to the human species
than to the humming-birds, provides her author with
the key that unlocks the profoundest of all realities:
the reality of the soul, of the aspiring and beauty-
craving soul, the soul that reaches out toward the un-
reachable loveliness which is at the rainbow's end, and
in still blue lakes, and in the deeper blue of human
eyes.

How such ardent beauty-worship could find utterance
in a less imaginative tale is more than I for one can con-

ceive. It is true, of course, that not all our writers
are W. H. Hudsons, and not all are filled with the same
impassioned devotion to the splendors of field and forest
and the subtler splendors within the heart of man.
Yet I suspect that many are turning deliberately and
even a little scornfully from that method which alone
offers them a chance for adequate expression; and I
fear that not a little of the legitimate material of the
unleashed imagination is made the slave of the wheel
of sodden fact.

Let us examine, for example, the difference in effect
between the objective and the imaginative methods in
dealing with one of the most commonplace of poetic subjects: the subject of lilacs. The first excerpt is from
the work of Amy Lowell, one of the best known writers
of the Literal school. The selection opens as follows:

> Lilacs,
> False blue,
> White,
> Purple,
> Color of lilac,
> Your great puffs of flowers
> Are everywhere in this my New England

and continues in this vein:

You were everywhere.
You tapped the window when the preacher preached his
    sermon,
And ran along the road beside the boy going to school.
You stood by pasture bars to give the cows good milking,
You persuaded the house-wife that her dish-pan was of silver
And her husband an image of pure gold.

You flaunted the fragrance of your blossoms
Through the wide doors of Custom Houses—
You, and sandal-wood, and tea,
Charging the noses of quill-driving clerks
When a ship came in from China.

The second poem is by Brian Hooker, also a contemporary poet, but one who holds to the older traditions. That Mr. Hooker has looked upon the lilacs
with imagination is evident when he writes:

You myriads of little litanies!
    Not as our bitter piety, subdued
To cold creed that denies
    Or lying law that severs glad and good;
But like a child's eyes, after sleep
    Uplifted; like a girl's first wordless prayer
    Close-held by him who loves her—no distress
Nor storm of supplication, but a deep,
    Dear heartache of such utter happiness
As only utter purity can bear. . . .

O sweet, sweet, sweet! You are the proof of all
    That over-truth our dreams have memory of
That day cannot recall;
    Work without weariness, and tearless love,
And taintless laughter. While we run
To measure dust, and sounding names are hurled
    Into the nothingness of days unborn,
You hold your little hearts up to the sun,
    Quietly beautiful amid our scorn—
God's answer to the wisdom of this world.

A comparison between Miss Lowell's work and Mr.
Hooker's is scarcely necessary. The first not only

takes root in observation, but is built up almost entirely
of observed fact; the second likewise has a basis in what
the author has seen, but is constructed almost exclusively of what he has imagined.   And does his imagination bear him further from reality than Miss
Lowell is borne by her realism?   Who would contend
that he has not shown a deeper penetration, a clearer
insight into the world's heart, a keener and subtler ability to interpret and present that which constitutes the
essence of life?

Now let us take still other examples; let us examine
two selections that treat a theme suitable for the most
radical of literary revolutionaries—the theme of steam
shovels.   Here is a passage from Eunice Tietjens' description of the steam monster:

> The iron head,
> Set on a monstrous jointed neck,
> Glides here and there, lifts, settles on the red
> Moist floor, with nose dropped in the dirt, at beck
> Of some incredible control.
> He snorts, and pauses couchant for a space;
> Then slowly lifts, and tears the gaping hole
> Yet deeper in earth's flank.   A sudden race
> Of loosened earth and pebbles trickles there
> Like blood-drops in a wound.
> But he, the monster, swings his load around—
> Weightless it seems as air.
> His mammoth jaw
> Drops widely open with a rasping sound,
> And all the red earth vomits from his maw.

From the point of view of accuracy this is not bad;
nor is it by any means lacking in vividness and imagina-

tion.   Yet how much less imaginative is it, and conse-
quently how much less impressive, than the following
sonnet, by Hugh Wilgus Ramsaur:

GARGANTUA

(*To a Steam Shovel*)

Like some lost monster of the Saurian Age
Forever made mechanical, you seem;
Steel-scaled, steel-boweled, belching clouds of steam,
Swooping to gore the earth with seething rage,
A fuming pterodactyl in a cage . . .
And yet I'm told you breathe a mighty dream
To scale the air with mortar, brick and beam,
And leave mankind a nobler heritage!

Your clanking, muddy jaws—the wounded soil,
Tell me that soon will rise another tower
Where, hidden from the sun, more gold will pass
And, buried from the world, more men will toil. . . .
Turning away, I see a broken flower—
And stone on stone and glass on leaden glass.

In the above poem the author makes use of modern
science, or, rather, of one of the products of modern
science; but it is not often that the work of our en-
gineers or chemists offers the stimulus for such successful literary activity.   Indeed, it is unquestionable that
one of the prime reasons for the present submergence of
the imagination is the rise of the scientific spirit, and
particularly of the scientific method.   For science—or,
at least, the uninspired science of every day—is painstaking and cautious in its ways; it takes account only

of detail and of fact; it is not concerned with that which cannot be known or ascertained, but leaves it for the discoverer or the genius to make prodigious flights into the heart of an electron or out across the imponderable ether of space.

The typical writer, unfortunately, is influenced by the average rather than by the exceptional scientist; he is affected far more by the physicist's prosy and logical analysis of visible effects than by the astronomer's poetic excursion into the invisible; mathematics and precise measurements are for him the symbols of science far more than a bold speculation and the charting of the wondrous and the unexplored.   Caring little or nothing for science for its own sake and having no conception of its broader and more fascinating aspects, our realist is likely to retain the impress of all that is leaden, dull and cut-and-dried, while the real founts of scientific inspiration will be closed to him as totally as the founts of poetic inspiration are closed to the average stock broker.

For in the case of science, as in so many other cases affecting modern literature, we meet with a startling contradiction.   Actually, science stands forth as the foe of literature because of its restraint upon the imagination; potentially, it is one of literature's stanchest allies because of the imaginative stimulus it might offer. Contrary to the general impression, science does not circumscribe and curtail the universe; instead, it widens and expands our conception of existing things to a point utterly beyond the comprehension of the most

audacious-minded of our predecessors.   No mythology
that was ever created, no historical episode that was
ever told, no tales of knights or warriors or heroes or
gods, offer half the imaginative or romantic possibilities
of modern science—when science is properly regarded.

How, for example, could the legendary heavens of the
ancients compare with the heavens of post-Copernican
astronomy, that infinite waste wherein flaming suns by
the million, and possibly millions of inhabited worlds,
go whirling at prodigious speeds on inexorable courses?
How could the magic revelations of storied sorcerers and
sages compare with the profounder revelations of modern physicists, who picture that infinitesimal unit, the
atom, as being a sort of miniature Solar System, with a
central neucleus about which the revolving electrons fly
like planets?   Or in what way could the marvels of old
miracle-workers equal those of modern biology, and in
particular of that natural history which tells of the incredible creatures dwelling in desert, meadow and wood
—bower-birds that arrange their nests with a genuine
esthetic sense, wasps that paralyze their victims and
leave them helpless as provender for the unborn, ants
that form living chains for scaling steep escarpments,
and a thousand other creatures with habits as intriguing
and extraordinary?

All this material, though it would seem to offer opportunities unbounded for the imaginative writer, has
been but little regarded in modern literature.   Occasionally, indeed, a Jules Verne has utilized some part
of it to weave an entertaining story, and now and then

an H. G. Wells has made of it the narrative vehicle for
vital ideas.   But few professional fiction writers have
employed it with the same imaginative vigor and effectiveness as has a professional scientist, Camille Flam-
marion, whose romance, *Urania,* is a magnificent philosophical narrative that takes us in a dream-flight up to
Mars and beyond the known borders of the starry universe, so casting a light of vivid speculation upon some
of the darkest problems of this world and of the cosmos,
of death and life and of the after-life.

Our poets, like our prose writers, have occasionally,
although rarely, borne us into this little trodden realm
of science.   The path that might be followed has been
indicated by Masefield in some of his sonnets, and by
George Sterling in his stately poem, *The Testimony of
the Suns,* which effectively presents an important philosophy based upon an imaginative interpretation of
the flaring of comets, the whirling of suns, and the cir-
cling of galaxies.   Something of the spirit of the latter
poem, and something of its method of linking science to
life by means of imagination, may be gleaned from the
following representative stanzas, which refer to the
hope of finding a solution to the eternal Why of the
universe:

> So dreamt thy sons on worlds destroyed
>   Whose dust allures our careless eyes,
>   As, lit at last on alien skies,
> The meteor melts athwart the void.
>
> So shall thy seed on worlds to be,
>   At altars built to suns afar,

> Crave from the silence of the star
> Solution of the mystery;
>
> And crave unanswered, till, denied
>> By cosmic gloom and stellar glare,
>> The brains are dust that bore the pray'r
> And dust the yearning lips that cried.

But the modernistic way of dealing with science is to overlook its imaginative implications and to treat it with the detailed accuracy of a text-book, according to the practice of one of our younger bards in the poem beginning, "Hark ye! ye slaves of inhibition!", or of Edgar Lee Masters in this characteristic passage:

> I lectured last night upon the morbus sacer
> Of falling sickness, epilepsy, of old
> In Palestine or Greece, so much ascribed
> To deities or devils.   To resume
> We find it caused by morphological
> Changes of the cortex cells.   Sometimes,
> More times, indeed, the anatomical
> Basis, if one be, escapes detection.
> For many functions of the cortex are
> Unknown, as I have said.
>
>   And now remember
> Mercier's analysis of heredity:
> Besides direct transmission of unstable
> Nervous systems, there remains the law
> Hereditary of sanguinity.

And so the author continues for four pages, thereby illustrating what may be termed the rational method in modern literature, a method that derives from the rationalism of science and that makes reason and known fact its gods as opposed to the unharnessed fancy of the romantics.

Regarding this rationalism it may be well to speak more than a word, for it is an influence as paralyzing as it is significant. It would make the poet's wings keep pace with the reagents in the chemical test-tubes, and would limit literary creativeness according to the shifting index of the laboratory. In other words, it would provide an extension of the laws of Visibility and of Surface Values, which we have already discussed; it would confine the subject matter of literature to that which is seen or ascertained, and would mark "Forbidden" across all those wide areas which have not yet received the scientific sanction.

Thus, while it would be permissible for a novelist to trace the descent of his characters according to Mendelian laws or to follow the suggestions of modern psychiatry by depicting dissociated or multiple personalities, it would be beyond the author's province to imagine and to illustrate new laws of heredity or to portray personalities distorted in ways unknown to psychological investigation. Again, if the writer were a believer in spiritualism, the rationalist would issue him no license to embody his faith in a creative work until spiritualism had received the official stamp of approval; and if he were so mid-Victorian as to believe in such an entity as the soul and that entity had not been passed by the scientific board of censorship, then he would forfeit the respect of all intelligent persons if he persisted in expressing his views.

For the attitude of science is fundamentally one of negation; nothing exists which has not been proved to exist.   And from the point of view of scientific experimentation such an attitude may be desirable, but from the point of view of literary creation it is little short of lethal, particularly since the form it often takes is: "Nothing can exist which has not been proved to exist."   If the human spirit cannot be isolated under the microscope, then the human spirit is unreal; if immortality cannot be subjected to quantitative analysis, then immortality is a myth and an illusion.   Such is the rationalism of science, or at least of that science which tends toward the mechanistic view of life and which seems most profoundly to have affected our younger writers.

But it does not require any extraordinary insight to demonstrate that such a rationalism is in reality highly irrational.   There is an obvious logical fallacy in denying the existence of that which one has not seen or known simply because one has not seen or known it; in some ways, this is but the reverse of that superstition which assumes the reality of such invisible forces as goblins and ghosts.   According to the tenets of present-day rationalists, the men of a thousand years ago were justified in supposing that the world was flat, that the sun revolved about the earth, and that our planet was the center and focus of the universe.   To imagine that our globe was but an isolated speck in immensity would then have been highly irrational, for where was the evidence to prove so extravagant a contention? Yet in time such evidence was forthcoming, and so the unreasonable was converted into the reasonable, and fields once open only to the giddy romanticist became legitimate territory for sober men of thought.

And may it not be the same with present-day conceptions? May not the most reckless theories, now deemed too irrational for serious consideration, become proved and so be made rational? May there not be whole universes hidden in the earth or air or in the ether of space, universes to be unbared before the scientists of a later age? And may not such realms even now be legitimate subjects for literary treatment?

For should the pen of the poet be excluded simply because the measuring rod of the scientist is too clumsy for admission? It is my belief—and in this I may be violently opposed by the rationalists—that the creative imagination may step in at any spot where scientific verification cannot tread; that when any subject remains in doubt and beyond the grasp of scientific inquiry, the writer may choose his own interpretation; that he may assume the existence or the non-existence of the soul, the transiency or the immortal reality of love, the annihilation of the human personality upon death or its perpetual reincarnation, its eventual penetration of the mysteries of life and fate or its everlasting bewilderment and despair.

But it is precisely at this point that our writers of the

realistic school follow too doggedly in the footsteps of science. The limitations of science become their limitations; its shortness of sight becomes their shortness of sight; its errors are their errors, its caution their caution, and its plodding ways their plodding ways. Since it despises that imagination which vaults beyond the touch of test-tube and beaker, they too are hearty in their contempt for imaginative effort. The result is that their work tends to become flat and barren, prosy and uninspiring, methodical as the thermometer and dry as the sands of the desert. And so we have work such as Edgar Lee Masters' disquisition on the "morbus sacer," quoted above, and novels built up at far greater length upon themes as dull; whereas the best literature of the present, and the greatest literature of all time, is the product of writers who have plunged free of the restraints of a narrow rationalism and have dared to imagine things so far from the demonstration of science as

The splendors of the firmament of time

or

The wind of death's imperishable wing

or

That Light whose smile kindles the Universe,
That Beauty in which all things work and move.

Closely related to the present-day scorn of the imaginative is the disregard of the beautiful, since beauty in

many of its manifestations is the offspring of the imagination, and in any event is in danger of being starved
and shriveled to death where imagination is lacking.
How Beauty as a literary divinity has been discredited
and overshadowed, and how in some cases Ugliness has
been deliberately established in the abandoned temple,
will form the subject of the following chapter.

CHAPTER VI

THE REPUDIATION OF THE BEAUTIFUL

WHEN the last echoes and tremors of the literary revolution have died away and the whole affair has assumed the remoteness of history, probably no phase of it will impress our successors as more curious than our attitude toward beauty. In a previous chapter we stated that "the present period has been witnessing an esthetic decline as marked as the growth of rationalism"; and while some aspects of that decline will be apparent from the foregoing quotations, the phenomenon is so wide-reaching and fraught with so many vital implications that it would elude comprehension unless considered in detail.

Even did we not know that the modern tendency has been to sully and obscure the beautiful, we might suspect as much from our knowledge of modern life. Can violets thrive in the reeking atmosphere of a garbage heap? Can lilies spring to bloom in an alley between gray stone walls? Then how expect that rarer flower—literary beauty—to burgeon out of the dust, the soot and the haste of factory and office? Amid the box-like buildings of a modern city, where trolleys jangle and motors honk and hurried crowds push and shove, what could be more remote than thought of "a glow-worm golden in a dell of dew" or "The light that never was on sea or land"?

Is it not far easier, and far more natural, to write in the vein of Carl Sandburg of the "City of the big shoulders" or of "any streetful of people buying clothes and groceries"?   Less uplifting, perhaps, but certainly far more in tune with the life that we live and observe!—certainly, the nearest approach to beauty encouraged by that bustling and strident environment wherein the greater number of our artists abide!   To the average man, "clothes and groceries" are among the outstanding facts of life—and is it not fitting that they should be outstanding facts for the poet as well? For we are living, as we have already remarked, in a material age; and materialism and beauty make as good bedfellows as fire and ice.   Indeed, the one exists almost in inverse proportion to the other; and the fact that some beauty still trickles occasionally to the light, particularly among our less progressive poets, is to be taken as proof that the power of materialism is not yet supreme.

But that it is threatening to become supreme will be evident to every follower of modern literature— with the possible exception of those who cannot see further back than the past ten or fifteen years.   In a previous chapter we mentioned how our people and our writers are bowing down at the shrine of that invisible deity, Millions of Dollars, and we indicated how that god has forbidden all worship of his arch-enemies, the sunset, the meadows, and the stars; but we did not show how thorough have been his conquests, nor by what subtle and crafty methods he has been driving out the foe.

For the campaigns of the great god Gold, and of all the minor divinities of the Hard-and-Fast, the Concrete and the Visible, have not been waged by obvious methods nor in the open. The ramparts of beauty, although seemingly fashioned of mere moonlight and mist, are so ancient that a direct assault would arouse a storm of resentment, and so stout that they might not yield to the aggressors. Therefore it is necessary for the assailants to resort to roundabout and unapparent tactics. And this they do by pretending reverence for the object of their attack. Under the guise of friendship they approach the citadel where Loveliness has sat enthroned since before Homer; and with heads deferentially unbared they enter, while under their mantles the rapiers and revolvers lie in waiting. But all is peaceful until the concealing walls are about them; then, with a few swift concerted strokes, they leap from behind upon the ancient guardians of the altar, fling them to the floor, gag and bind them, and cast them out of the windows. And at the same time they cast out Loveliness, the old Loveliness adored by Dante and Milton and Shakespeare; and in her place they crown a new Loveliness, or at least a sovereign whom they name Loveliness, although her face is hag-like and misshapen. Then, since the victory has been won behind closed doors and far from the world's sight, they deny that there has even been a battle, but boldly proclaim, "Beauty is still our goddess," and temper their announcement by adding, "It is a newer and a more vital Beauty."

But the curious fact is that, while beauty has been deposed, there is no general admission of her dethronement. The power of the old tradition is too great to be shattered completely; the only choice is to create a new tradition, and to plead in favor of a "new beauty." Thus we find that, while many of our writers are scornful or intolerant of that which the esthetic sense of their predecessors has endorsed, they will not openly acknowledge their belief and perhaps are not even fully conscious of it, but appeal for a new esthetic creed that shall be adapted to the taste and life of a new age. Their method is either to give the name "Beauty" to that which no writer of a previous era would have thought of calling beautiful, or else to exalt some limited and minor phase of beauty at the expense of its broader and more essential elements. They would have us believe that they hold with Keats that

> A thing of beauty is a joy forever

or that

> Beauty is truth, truth beauty: that is all
> Ye know on earth, and all ye need to know,

and yet they despise the very thing that Keats and his kindred treasured most highly, and turn from the "realms of gold" and the sweetness of "unheard melodies" to a woman "with a hairpin in her teeth" or "Candles guttering sideways in tomato cans."

It is no doubt true that "a rose by any other name would smell as sweet," but it is also undeniable that a cabbage by any other name would smell like a cabbage. The modern practice is to discard the flowers and to give the cabbages a large-lettered label, "Roses"! And since this nomenclature is agreed upon by the best critical authority, there can be no disputing the verdict, but our cabbages must henceforth be esteemed for their rare colors and their fragrance.

In order to illustrate the meaning of beauty in the eyes of the modernists, let me quote briefly from Amy Lowell's *Tendencies in Modern American Poetry*.

"All that one can safely say of Mr. Sandburg's work," she declares, in her summary of that writer's achievement, "is that it contains touches of great and original beauty." And, in order to prove her point, she quotes verses of which the following lines are typical:

I am riding on a limited express, one of the crack trains
    of the nation.

Now the stone house on the lake front is finished and the
    workmen are beginning the fence.

I have been watching the war map slammed up for adver-
    tising in front of the newspaper office.
Buttons—red and yellow buttons—blue and black buttons—
    are shoved back and forth across the map.

If this be beauty, then how beauty has changed

since Shelley, writing one of the most magnificent
of his lyrics on this ancient and inexhaustible theme,
was led to sing:

> The awful shadow of some unseen Power
> Floats, though unseen, amongst us,—visiting
> This various world with as inconstant wing
> As summer winds that creep from flower to flower.

Certainly, the unseen Power of which Shelley sang
remains unseen! Not even its "inconstant wing" can
be heard flickering from flower to flower; it has apparently fled entirely for realms unknown, except when
at times its pinions tremulously beat among the despised lovers of an obsolescent beauty. The "awful
shadows" of a vast and intangible majesty may have
been all very well for a previous age, when men still
had time for idle dreaming and there was no chance
to picture the graceful lines of six-cylinder Sedans
and the elegance of electric advertising signs. But
we have now outlived the crudity of the days of Shelley.
For do we not dwell in the illumination of shadow-
quenching arc-lights, and do we not show a superior
sensitiveness by seeing beauty all around us in the
glare of our street traffic and above us in the roofs
of our skyscrapers or the wings of our airplanes?

So, at least, the modern might be expected to ask
while showing his poetic sense by telling us that he
"drank musty ale at the Illinois Athletic Club" or
"sat with a dynamiter at supper in a German saloon
eating steak and onions." But, fortunately, the con-

temporary conception of beauty is a broad one, and does not confine itself to splendors such as these. It is even able at times to embrace expressions which the limited taste of our predecessors might have been able to recognize as mildly beautiful; and there are a few of our writers who devote themselves assiduously to the pretty presentation of trivialities, to a sort of toying with things of no intrinsic importance in order to deck them doll-like in colorful garments. Even so, however, the doll garments must be colorful in a new way; there must be some distinguishing tint or shade, preferably something glaring and noticeable; and, thanks to this element of novelty, the product is likely to be applauded as High Art or High Beauty by the modernists, although in truth it has little in common with that "awful Loveliness" to whom Shelley vowed to dedicate his powers.

Examples of this limited and merely decorative beauty are not hard to find. One might offer numerous illustrations from the work of Amy Lowell, H. D., John Gould Fletcher and their fellow Imagists. But the following, by Mr. Fletcher, will serve as well as any other:

When the moon lights up
Its dull red camp-fire through the trees;
And floats out, like a white balloon,
Into the blue cup of the night, borne by a casual breeze;
The moon-orchestra begins to stir:
Jiggle of fiddles commence their crazy dance in the dark-
    ness

Crickets churr
Against the stark reiteration of the rusty flutes. . . .

In quoting this excerpt, it is not my purpose to criticize the technique; to comment upon the tangled images or upon the incongruity of the lighter of a camp-fire floating out like a balloon, or of an object so vast as a balloon gliding into a receptacle so small as a cup. Such confusion is common enough among writers of the decorative school. It is merely my desire to point out that whole poems and whole long prose passages are made up of such descriptions, and that these descriptions seem to embody the highest modernistic idea of Beauty.

I might observe, moreover, that members of the decorative group are guilty of a sort of inverted vision; are proponents of a topsy-turvey art which to a broad understanding would have all the elements of comedy, since it places the bottom of the picture where the top should be and the rear in the proper place of the front. In other words, they emphasize that which is least in need of emphasis, and obscure that which is most vital; they identify the part with the whole, and mistake the instrument for the accomplishment; they shove ornamentation forward so as to make it seem the end rather than the means of art: which is like devoting all one's attention to the color of the wall paper in one's home, and paying no heed to the solidity of the wall. For literature—if it be good literature—is after all a more or less solid product; all the

gilding and garnishing of the artist's brush can be
only incidental to the completion of the main design;
and to confuse that gilding and garnishing with the
main design is to make the product a rococo and tinsel thing.

But this is not to imply that beauty should not have
a primary place in artistic creation. It is only to plead
against that debased and minor beauty which centers
about petty and inconsequential things; which cannot
feel the breath of free winds, nor the sweep of an un-
chained magnificence; which is master in a merely
pretty bird's nest house of art instead of being an attendant in the corridors of the soul. True, the idea of
the soul has fallen into disfavor of late, largely owing
to an unimaginative rationalism. But, at the risk of
appearing woefully orthodox, I propose to use this term
with reference to whatever it is in man that thinks,
feels or imagines and to that extent does not resemble
the stone or the clod; I shall take the position that
this intangible entity is the fountain of all beauty, and
that only under the stimulus of beauty can it be fully
unfolded.

It is this belief that brings me into conflict with
those who conceive of beauty as a sort of pleasant toy,
a trinket with which to do clever tricks or idle away
a dull hour or two. I cannot help feeling that such
persons are doing far worse than merely to dawdle
away their time; they are playing the traitor to whatever is best in themselves and in life. It may be that
they have been momentarily blinded, or that their

minds are clogged and blunted by the too heavy atmosphere of practical affairs; but, at all events, it seems to me that the materialism of our iron cities must have infected them as it has infected so many millions and narrowed the circle of their perceptions to that which they share in common with the dog, the ox and the beetle—to the things of sense, of bulk and weight and of ascertainable practical value. And these are precisely the things in whose presence the beautiful cannot endure. For beauty has its seat not in the objective or conscious self but in the subjective or deeper personality; it makes its appeal to those parts of the mind which are ordinarily overshadowed; it strikes down beneath the level of the subconscious, lifts the veil from whole vast psychic areas of which we are not usually aware, and thereby arouses one's whole being to fuller life and activity, opens the way for the emergence of all that is timeless within us, and fuses the individuality with the unchangeable and the eternal.

Consider for example, the effect that may be produced by music,—let us listen in imagination to a violin solo. Before the performer takes up his bow, one may be conscious of such concrete facts as that one is sitting on an upholstered seat in a crowded hall, and that the man at one's left is rather too plump and has red hair; but at the first note one may find one's self summoned into another universe. And if the piece and the playing and one's own mood so conspire, one may gradually be borne further and further away upon the waves of harmonious sound; one may enter a realm where upholstered seats and one's stout neighbor and the crowded hall do not exist; one may be sad at griefs one has never known, be uplifted at exaltations one has never felt, dream dreams that one has never dreamt before; one may drift far back in the past to that moment which seems to embrace all moments, and glide far into the future till one looks upon eternity as upon an open plain; one may be filled with yearnings that seem to come to one from across all the ages, and with regrets and sorrows that are as the sorrows of the universe itself, and finally with that peace and that consolation which heal all injuries, atone for all sufferings, and assure one of the everlasting harmony of all things.

Then—after a period that our clocks may measure as a mere five or ten minutes—the music will throb to an end, its bewitching spell will fade away, and the world of padded seats and crowded humanity will return. But what will have happened in the interval? Would it not be correct to say that, under the prompting of beauty, one had become a different being,— that one's mind had burst out of the crust of earthly things, had been released into new and exhilarating realms, perhaps had even clutched at the keys of the ultimate truths?

For there can be no doubt that beauty alters the focus of the soul, concentrates its attention upon realities to which we are ordinarily blind, and so offers a criterion of truth which, while sheerly intuitive, may be more reliable than the palpably erroneous criterion

of sense.   It may seem extravagant to state that we can
know the world only by apprehending that which is
beautiful in life and in art; but I feel convinced that,
if our existence be anything more than a raucous and
wholly external striving after bread and butter, bank
notes and bonds, then no comprehension of its true
nature and no fulfillment of its ultimate functions, can
be gained without the teachings of beauty.

It was perhaps something of this sort that Wordsworth had in mind when he wrote:

> Thanks to the human heart by which we live,
> Thanks to its tenderness, its joys and fears,
> To me the meanest flower that blows can give
> Thoughts that do often lie too deep for tears.

It is to be noted that the poet chose as his symbol
a flower—a beautiful thing.   And it is probable that
his choice was unconscious rather than deliberate; no
doubt he did not have to hesitate and debate with himself whether, instead of "flower," he should employ the
word "squirrel" or "turnip" or "spinach."

"Of course not!" the reader will reply.   "Turnip
or spinach would be simply ridiculous!"   Very true!—
but why ridiculous?   Not because in themselves they
are ridiculous plants; merely because, not being beautiful, they are inconsistent with the poet's idea, and
because subconsciously we recognize the inconsistency,
subconsciously we understand that only things of
beauty can draw upon the hidden reserves of the spirit,

and thereby, through opening up the gates of the subjective self, can arouse "thoughts that do often lie too deep for tears."

It is precisely at this point that Wordsworth and his modern successors clash. Evidently the latter would see no objection to writing "turnip" or "spinach" where he has written "flower." Indeed, "spinach" might be vastly preferred by certain of the group, for "flower" is an old and hackneyed term, whereas spinach is—poetically speaking—comparatively novel and fresh. True, it is by no means a beautiful expression, and its connotations are not beautiful; but that, in the eyes of the moderns, might also be an advantage, for they have come to adopt an unavowed Cult of the Ugly and thereby to avoid the danger of the cliché; and so far have they carried their advances that onions—or turnips or spinach—are now of more literary utility than lilies, and the odor of the wash-line than the odor of the rose.

The quotations I have already offered will make it unnecessary to dwell upon this point. But what I particularly wish to note is that many members of the present school appear to be so sense-bound as to have no conception of "thoughts that do often lie too deep for tears" or of the underlying beauty that makes such thoughts possible. Only the visible and the material appears to project itself into their world, and therefore they perhaps feel that anything visible or material is a suitable subject for art; which is a little as if, at the violin solo that we have just imagined, there were to be an accompaniment of motor horns and tin cans. I am told, indeed, that something of this sort has been attempted in modern music; and while not prepared to pass judgment upon it, I should not be surprised to find it a parallel to what has been undertaken in literature, the product of the same clamorous social conditions and of the same soul-suffocating materialism.

At any rate, I feel convinced that, while a few jaded and eccentric minds might find a certain pleasure even in the rattling of dish-pans or the smashing of crockery, they would not derive the same esthetic satisfaction as he who finds himself uplifted and borne away by the quavering, ecstatic melody of the violin.

And it is to the rattling dish-pan, crockery-smashing sort of literature that I most seriously object. Let those that wish enjoy this particular form of entertainment; let them make all the noise they will, like a group of roistering college boys; let them even go so far as to array themselves and their works to resemble a parade of Solomon Island head hunters—but let them not call their farce grand opera, nor seek to have their screams and yells acknowledged as song, nor go clamoring after the scalps of those of us who still search for beauty on the old and trodden pathways. No doubt we are a little out of date in looking to mere loveliness for a revelation of life's profoundest meaning and purpose; but through loveliness, to quote Wordsworth once more,

We feel that we are greater than we know

and so aspire to read

the eternal deep
Haunted forever by the eternal mind

while our more progressive contemners prefer to find
esthetic consummation by writing of "fawn-tinged hos-
pital pajamas" or of

Complacencies of the peignoir, and late
Coffee and oranges in a sunny chair

or else regale themselves to the tune of

Rum tiddy um
tiddy um
tiddy um tum tum
My knees are loose-like, my feet want to sling themselves,
I feel like tickling you under the chin—honey—and a-asking:
Why does a Chicken Cross the Road?

CHAPTER VII

THE POETIC ANARCHY

O Poet, then, forbear
　The loosely sandalled verse,
Choose rather thou to wear
　The buskin—straight and terse;

Leave to the tyro's hand
　The limp and shapeless style,
See that thy form demand
　The labor of the file.

—Austin Dobson

IN the three previous chapters we have considered certain of the effects of the literary revolution upon the spirit of contemporary poetry and prose. We have discussed the current outburst of realism, the efflorescence of the Literal and of the Psychological, the rise of the Scientific, the Material and the Rational, and the simultaneous discouragement of all that is imaginative and beautiful. But we have yet to give our close attention to recent transformations in form, which, as we have indicated, are as notable as the changes in spirit and subject matter, and are inextricably connected with those changes. So important are they, indeed, that—even if we confine our remarks on impressionism and expressionism to those we have already made—we will hardly be able to dismiss the topic in less than two chapters.

And since the subject divides itself logically into halves, we will begin with a consideration of innovations in poetic form, and will reserve the following chapter for an examination of the altered basis of prose style.

When we approach the theme of poetry, we at once find ourselves in disputed territory. Among the first volunteers for the literary revolution have been our versifiers; for more than a decade already the flag of rebellion has been waving, and the battle has been raging between the old school of poets and the new. In Great Britain, it is true, the conflict has never been so severe as in America, and the rebels have never been so near to ransacking the ancient strongholds; but even in Great Britain the struggle has burst out in certain quarters, while in the United States the revolutionists have entrenched themselves powerfully in the soil of their foes, have won engagement after engagement, and have been threatening to batter down the resisting fortifications with their salvos of alleged verse.

What, then, is the contest all about? As in the case of so many other wars, the struggle is for liberty: the insurrectionists cry out that they have been imprisoned in rules; they insist that we must win independence of convention, or that the lyric muse will die. In a word, free verse has been announcing itself as poetry. And while modest enough not to claim to be the only poetry, it ascribes numerous virtues to itself alone. Release from artificial restrictions is its loudest battle cry; it seeks emancipation from the trammels of rhyme and of meter; it plans to throw established rules to the four winds, in favor of rules of its own making; it desires to create beauty without respect to the recognized principles of beauty, to compose poetry in disregard of the traditional poetic essentials. All this is a laudable aim, provided that it succeeds—but can it succeed? Like other rebels, the poetic insurgents are to be judged by their success; and if they can establish that theirs are the true poetic essentials, while the principles that governed Milton, Shelley and Tennyson are defective, then the wreaths of victory will be theirs, and the Gray's "Elegy" and the "Prometheus Unbound" of the future will be composed in free verse.

At the outset, I do not deny that the free versifiers have produced something in the way of literature. But not all literature is poetry. And therein, it seems to me, the poetic radicals are guilty of a basic misconception.

If Mark Twain, as a bit of whimsical humor, had chopped one of his prose articles into fantastic form, commenced each line with a capital letter, and labeled the whole poetry, he would have been attempting in jest what some of the writers of today are undertaking seriously. And if he had declared that in so doing he was guided by rules known only to himself, and that the ear which could take pleasure in Shelley and Swinburne was not always delicate enough to value him correctly, he would have been foreshadowing the attitude of the free versifiers. The difference is that he would have been greeted with laughter, whereas the free versifiers are sometimes accorded a more sober approval.

Yet Mark Twain's work might have been literature. The joke would have consisted in calling it poetry.

Now whether they know it or not, the *vers librists* are perpetrating a tremendous joke. There is nothing they cannot stamp as poetry, so long as they give it a "jagged appearance"; they have taken singularity of form as the chief poetical criterion, and there are many who accept this criterion without even a smile. I confess that it does not make all the difference in the world what a thing is called: that literature will not come to an end if we entitle prose poetry; and that the songs of Burns and the sonnets of Keats will survive unaffected even by the "polyphonic prose" of John Gould Fletcher and the Imagistic ebullitions of Ezra Pound. But if a hoax is being perpetrated, I believe in exposing that hoax; and if a group of poetic charlatans are drawing attention to themselves by juggling cleverly with words, I consider it right to say that they are charlatans. And it seems that a whole school of poets is imitating on a large scale the "Spectric Poems" of Witter Bynner and Arthur Davison Ficke, which were issued as a joke, yet were seriously commended by the critics.

Of course, the free verse writers will object to this. They will say that theirs is a perfectly legitimate attempt to create something new in poetry; that the mere incident of a difference in method should not cause their ostracism in the poetical community; and that it is most unjust to call them charlatans. They will resent the insinuation that they are even unconsciously the perpetrators of a hoax, and will complain that, like all great reformers, they are being abused and misunderstood; and because they are abused and misunderstood they will argue that they are great reformers.

In order to answer this plea, we must consider the nature of poetry in general and of free verse in particular, and seek to determine whether the two may be one and the same.

To begin with, it would be easy to dogmatize and to say that poetry is metrical expression. But all lovers of poetry must realize that this definition has not an unlimited application. If it had, many of our ephemeral outbursts of newspaper wit would be poetry, and *Mary's Little Lamb* would be as much a poem as Wordsworth's *She Dwelt Among the Untrodden Ways*, which is written in the same meter. On the other hand, no one can doubt that Wordsworth's *Intimations of Immortality* is as true a poem as was ever written, although it is irregular in form; or even that Matthew Arnold's *Philomela* is a poem, although it lacks both strict regularity and consistent rhyme.

Perhaps no better definition of poetry has ever been made than the famous statement of Wordsworth that it is "emotion recollected in tranquillity." And yet I believe that something has been added to this definition by Professor G. H. Palmer, in his interesting book on *Formative Types in English Poetry,* wherein he declares that poetry is a "fragment of reality seen through a temperament," or "the conscious transmission of an emotional experience to another imaginative mind," and that the test of poetry is "if it is beautiful or ugly, not if it is false or true."   The definition has been further analyzed and explained by Professor J. L. Lowes, in the admirable volume entitled *Convention and Revolt in Poetry,* in which he states that the end of art is "to stir us with the sense of an imperishable beauty," and that this can be accomplished only when "emotion recollected in tranquillity" has "touched the springs of the imagination."   Or, to put it more briefly, Professor Lowes declares that poetic truth is "illusion tinged with emotion."

By illusion is not to be understood anything that is false.   This word merely signifies that an illusion makes true for the reader that which is true for the poet; in other words, that the reader is transplanted into the poet's place, and accepts the poet's thoughts as his own.

If the above analyses be correct, the ingredients essential to poetry are, first, beauty, and second, illusion, produced by imaginative or emotional means.   And though, as we have seen, the element of beauty can hardly be over-valued, it is in some ways subservient to the illusion; its object, among other things, is to reënforce the illusion; to make the illusion possible; to create such an atmosphere that the emotions and the imaginings of others will be accepted as our own. The fundamental difference between poetry and prose is perhaps that poetry is more concerned with making true for the reader that which originally was true for the author alone. But this initial difference gives rise to another and no less important distinction, which is that the poet must have the use of every possible tool to convey to others that which for him is truth. And therein lies the justification of rhyme and rhythm.

To give my own definition of poetry would be beside the point. Definitions at best are arbitrary; they are rarely all-inclusive; and while intended to explain the truth, they often obscure it. But it will be impossible to proceed without admitting that in every definition of poetry the elements of beauty and of illusion must be included. As regards the first, there will be scarcely any dispute: even the high priests of the Cult of Ugliness do not openly deny beauty, and even the free versifiers at times aim to create beautiful things, although their esthetic views do not meet with universal acceptance. And probably there will be little question about the second; it is undeniable that many, if not all, of the great poems of the past have aimed to create illusion, and that their success has been proportional to the success of the illusion. And the object of present-day Imagists in striving for flash-light impressions may be summed up in one word—illusion.

Beauty in formal poetry has in large part been attained through two instrumentalities, rhyme and rhythm, supplemented by a number of subsidiary de-

vices, such as alliteration, assonance, *etc*. Of all these
contrivances, the only admittedly indispensable one
has been rhythm—and in conventional poetry, rhythm
has meant the recurrence at regular intervals of accented and unaccented syllables. But of late years a
new conception of rhythm has been crying for a hearing—and has received it. The free versifiers have
issued their Declaration of Independence from what
they conceive to be the hammering regularity of the
older poetry. They maintain that the true rhythm
may be varied freely at the author's discretion; that it
consists neither in lines of a given length, nor in feet
of a given length, but that it is governed by principles
of cadence, and that the poetical unit should be the
strophe. They have also formulated rules according
to which a line should be of a "breath-length"—though
it is far from apparent what a breath-length may be.
They adopt as their standard the rhythm of breathing;
but, unhappily, they seem to forget that nothing is
much more regular than normal breathing, and that the
one, two, one, two of our inhaling and exhaling is far
more monotonous than anything ever written by the
most monotonous rhymster.

Probably the free versifiers are right in attempting to
model their rhythm upon our breathing, for our breathing is so inherently a part of us that in all likelihood
our conception of rhythm is molded in accordance with
it—but what they overlook is that those poetical forms
to which they object are those most nearly akin to
natural breathing. The argument for lines based upon

the rhythm of breathing is one of the strongest arguments for the older poetry.

In abandoning the conception of rhythm as a regular succession of accented and unaccented feet, the *vers librists* seem to me to have made more than one fundamental oversight. For some reason which it is the function of the psychologist rather than the literary critic to explain, a regular succession of syllables of a given kind has the power of stamping itself forcefully upon the mind, so as to produce a pronounced effect of pleasure. This pleasure is one of the marks of what we term poetic beauty; and whenever it occurs, it is able to impress itself deeply upon the individual's consciousness, and to cut its way into his memory. In other words, it appeals to the subjective mind, and through the subjective mind exerts a profound influence upon the objective or conscious self. To this is to be attributed the comparative ease with which passages of poetry may be memorized and retained in the memory; and, more important, the initial emotional effect that poetry may produce. Poems which contain no outstanding word or passage, no distinctiveness of atmosphere and no thought not commonly expressed, may be capable of arousing the emotions to white heat, whereas the same sentiment, if embodied in prose, would leave the reader cold. And the reason is that the regular rhythm reënforces the thought, stamps itself upon the mind with an impression of beauty, and through beauty aids in unfolding the full meaning of the passage and developing all its latent possibilities.

If we analyze the poems of the past that depart from a strict metrical scheme, we will find that those that approach nearest to true poetry are the most regular in rhythm. I have already characterized Arnold's *Philomela* as a poem, in spite of its apparent irregularity; let us now examine it more closely. Take the following stanza, which is typical of the whole:

> Dost thou tonight behold
> Here through the moonlight on this English grass,
> The unfriendly palace in the Thracian wild?
> Dost thou again peruse
> With hot cheeks and sear'd eyes
> The too clear web, and thy dumb Sister's shame?

It is apparent that underlying the whole is a regular iambic rhythm. The selection contains not a single foot that is not either a legitimate iambus, or else a legitimate variation of the iambus, permissible even in the strictest of verse forms. But that is far from all. The passage is composed of three five-foot iambic lines and three three-foot lines—and he who knows anything of prosody, knows that lines of these lengths blend excellently. If this poem were rhymed, no one would dream of calling it free, except in the sense that Wordsworth's *Intimations of Immortality* is free— and who will maintain that rhyme is essential to poetry?

In this connection, I may remark that when rhyme is attached to verse regarded as free, it seems to have a certain binding effect, an effect of correlating the lines in an orderly musical arrangement which might otherwise be lacking. And this may in large measure

explain why irregular rhymed compositions so much more frequently strike a true poetical note than irregular compositions without rhyme.

In connection with the above passage from Arnold, let us examine a selection from a contemporary free versifier. Consider the following, by Vachel Lindsay:

In the days of President Washington,
The glory of the nations,
Dust and ashes,
Snow and sleet,
And hay and oats and wheat,
Blew west,
Crossed the Appalachians,
Found the glades of rotting leaves, the soft deer-pastures,
The farms of the far-off future
In the forest.
Colts jumped the fence,
Snorting, ramping, snapping, sniffing,
With gastronomic calculations . . .

If there is any kind of poetic foot Mr. Lindsay has left out of these few lines, the omission may be explained as an oversight. The only regularity observable in this and scores of similar passages is a consistent irregularity; and if any one can discover in them a rhythm which is not that of prose, and of the most ordinary prose, he must indeed have an extraordinary ear.

In *Philomela* there is a clear reason for the division into lines. But can any one explain why Mr. Lindsay's offering should not be divided in any one of fifty ways?

Clearly, it lacks the rhythm of the line. And, more clearly yet, it lacks the underlying rhythmic scheme of equal foot-lengths which entitles *Philomela* to the name poetry. Is there not in this alone an adequate reason for calling the one passage prose, and the other poetry?

Now let us analyze two selections from another *vers librist*: Walt Whitman—the king of the free versifiers. Observe the following, the beginning of *The Mystic Trumpeter*:

Hark, some wild trumpeter, some strange musician,
Hovering unseen in air, vibrates capricious tunes tonight.
I hear thee, trumpeter, listening alert, I catch thy notes,
Now pouring, whirling, like a tempest round me,
Now low, subdued, now in the distance lost.

It does not require any straining of the rules of scansion to ascertain that these lines maintain a good iambic rhythm, with only those minor variations permissible even in rigid verse forms. And if one will take the trouble to read and analyze the rest of the poem, one will discover that the iambic norm is preserved until the end. Let the free versifiers not appeal to Whitman!

Here is a second selection—*The Last Invocation*:

At the last, tenderly,
From the walls of the powerful, fortressed house,
From the clasp of the knitted locks, from the keep of the well-
    closed doors,
Let me be wafted.

Let me glide noiselessly forth;
With the keys of softness unlock the locks—with a whisper
Set ope the doors O soul.

Tenderly—be not impatient,
(Strong is your hold, O mortal flesh,
Strong is your hold, O love.)

At the basis of this is an anapestic rhythm, which is varied liberally with iambic feet. But the anapest, whenever employed, may be frequently replaced by the iambus—and the above poem contains no more departures from the standard than occur in many poems regarded as regular. The effect of this impressive poem would be destroyed did not accented and unaccented syllables follow one another with approximate regularity—and it is the tacit recognition of the need for such regularity which elevates the work of Whitman above the ordinary level of prose.

However, there are some who maintain that the difference between poetry and prose consists in the manner of reading: that if a passage is printed so as to be read in one way, it will be prose, while if to be read in another way, it will be poetry. But we need not dwell upon this point, for though it is doubtless true that much importance attaches to vocal expression, still it is hard to believe that the manner of reading can explain the difference between Keats' "Ode on a Grecian Urn" and a present-day poet's dissertation on a bath tub.

When a passage is on the poetical border-line, good reading will perhaps serve to pull it across. But when it is not even within hailing distance of the border, good reading might as soon try to make a Ciceronian oration out of one of the harangues of Micawber.

Even aside from the liberties they take in reading prose as poetry, the most insistent cry of the new school of poets is freedom. And without endeavoring to show that the older poetry offers boundless opportunities for freedom and variety, and that hundreds of poets have found it free enough to write masterpieces in, I must remark that the *vers librists* are here overlooking another fundamental distinction between prose and poetry. Prose is the vehicle for the ordinary expression of ideas, poetry for their artistic expression. Artistic creation must always imply restraint; it must involve a certain sacrifice for the sake of effect; its function is to remold the gross material of inartistic expression into the sharply defined and chiseled product of art. A well made poem, according to the older standards, is such a chiseled product; it not only expresses the idea, and expresses it concisely, but presents it so as to give a maximum impression of beauty and to secure a maximum effect. In prose, on the other hand, the same idea might be expounded at great length; but, more important, it would not have such a sharpness of outline, it would not be enveloped in such an atmosphere of beauty. This fact seems never to occur at all to the free versifiers. They ask for freedom, and forget that freedom is not the way to art; they clamor to express an idea untrammeled by convention, and fail to remember that the only vehicle permitting such liberty is prose. They demand all the rights of the prose writer, and shrink from all the duties of the poet—and yet they call their productions poetry!

Still another fact overlooked by the poetic insurgents is that the rules of formal poetry are not always a hindrance; that often they are of invaluable assistance. The structure of any stanzaic form serves as a framework on which the poet can build; some such skeleton is as indispensable to certain poems as are the supporting girders to a modern skyscraper. Without a stanzaic form, Shelley's "Skylark" and Poe's "Raven" would alike be impossible; it is difficult indeed to imagine how a Poe or a Shelley could adapt himself to the limpness of free verse.

The sustained effect of an orderly rhythmical scheme is another instrumentality powerful in forcing a definite impression upon the mind; when skillfully employed, a succession of feet of the same kind produces an atmosphere either of profound gloom or of exuberant joy. How, for example, would the all-pervasive melancholy of "The Raven" be possible except through the dreary regularity of its trochaic rhythm? Or take the following from a contemporary writer—Charles Hanson Towne:

We were rushing through the valley, and my friend was at
    the wheel;
The highway lay before us like a rod of burnished steel.

There was dust upon our motor, there was dust before our eyes,
But the live thing sped like magic underneath the Summer skies.

Does this not produce exactly the required effect of swift motion? One can almost feel one's self in the motor car, rushing along the highway. And to what can we attribute this impression except to the dash of the pæonic rhythm, which bears one along literally with half-mile strides? Yet this sort of regularity is precisely what the free versifiers are striving to avoid.

Of course, they may argue that free verse is so flexible that they may employ any particular meter so long as the thought requires, and change at will to any other advantageous rhythm. But what would they do in the case of a poem whose sole theme was the racing of a motor car? They could not be effective without employing a regular anapestic or pæonic rhythm, with no greater variations than those permitted to the conventional versifier; and if they resorted to such a rhythm, they would be admitting the claims of formal poetry.

Beyond this, the free versifiers are rejecting a tool of enormous value when they refuse the aid of rhyme. While not indispensable, rhyme is at times of the utmost assistance to the poet. There is a reason why so many of the English poetic classics are rhymed; and that reason does not consist entirely in the decorative effect of corresponding line-endings. Such ornamentation, of course, may at times be an object in itself;

it is needless to argue that Tennyson's "Blow, Bugle, Blow" or Shelley's "Cloud" could not be the same without rhyme—but there are cases in which beauty is a secondary consideration, yet in which rhyme is employed to excellent advantage. Take the works of Pope—and try to imagine them without rhyme. Consider, for example, the couplet:

> Honor and shame from no condition rise:
> Act well your part; there all the honor lies.

Now reconstruct it without rhyme:

> Honor and shame from no condition rise:
> Act well your part; there all the honor rests.

The difference between the two couplets consists in a single word; the rhythm and the meaning are precisely the same in both cases. Yet what a difference of effect! The first stamps itself upon the mind, although not primarily as something beautiful; the second leaves comparatively little impression. And the reason is not hard to find. As beauty here is obviously of minor importance, rhyme is valuable less for the pleasure it gives than for its power of hammering the thought into the consciousness. This will explain why the most effective epigrams are rhymed; and, when considered in connection with the beauty of rhyme, it will account for the fact that it is so difficult to produce a successful unrhymed emotional poem.

The rhymes may be considered the ligaments of a poem. They bind it together; they link line securely

to line, and unify and coördinate the whole; they tie
the various segments of the stanza, as it were, into a
bundle, and give them the added strength of union.
Without this binding action, the effectiveness of many
of the English classics would be impossible; without
some adequate substitute, the free versifiers may have
difficulty in holding their poetry together.

In many respects, the free versifiers resemble the
ultra radicals in other fields.   They see something in
need of reform, and would tear down the entire structure of poetry in order to reform it, just as the political anarchists would utterly demolish the edifice of
the law in order to strike at certain evils with which
law is attended.   It is like blowing up a city in order
to get rid of a sidewalk.   I will admit that certain
things about conventional poetry would not suffer
from revision, and that certain of the aims of the *vers
librists* are undoubtedly in the right direction—the
trouble is that they are too far in the right direction;
that they fail to stop upon reaching their destination.
Four of the six aims of the Imagists, as stated by Miss
Lowell in *Tendencies in Modern American Poetry*, may
be conceded without dispute; hardly any one will deny
that poetry should always employ the right word, that
it should present an image, that it should be concentrated, and that it should not be blurred or indefinite.
But in order to attain these ends, one does not have to
dynamite the structure of the older poetry.

The essence of the poetical revolt consists in two of
the demands of the Imagists: the insistence upon new

rhythms and upon absolute freedom in the choice of subject. I think I have already sufficiently discussed the question of rhythm, but in this connection I may touch upon one point more. The Imagists base their objection to the old rhythms on the fact that they "echo old moods"—as if there were any moods that are not old! Love and hatred, joy and sorrow, anger, jealousy, desire—what moods are not variations upon these or upon other abiding emotions and passions? There is no mood that is not time-worn as human nature, no mood that was not ancient in the days of Sappho—and yet the poets of the twentieth century are preparing for new moods!

Regarding freedom in the choice of subject I do not think it necessary to say more than I have already stated in the chapters on realism, imagination and beauty. Let the poets select what subjects they wish—but let them remember that he who takes an unpoetical theme thereby passes his own death sentence. There is no surer way to write ephemeral poetry than to choose an ephemeral topic, and that poet whose subject is not one of the perennial sources of universal interest will be heard neither universally nor perennially. The manufacture of the 1927 model limousine, for example, may be fascinating to certain persons today, and there may at present be some who would gladly read a poem on this subject—yet no matter what the author's skill in versification, no matter how masterful his handling of detail and his descriptive power, the poem will be

short-lived as the present methods of automobile manufacture.

The demand for freedom in the choice of subject
evidently represents the reaction from the self-imposed
restriction of certain poets to the time-honored themes.
And, in the same way, the demands for the right word,
for concentration, and for definite images, are manifestations of the revolt against the vague, imitative
poems with which we have been deluged for years.
The old poetic ideas, expressed vaguely in the old
poetic diction and through the old poetic images, have
been poured forth in diluted form in such a torrent
as conceivably to give some an attack of nausea.   It
is not to the revolt against old abuses that I object;
it is not only that this revolt partakes of the character
of most rebellions in going too far, but that it has completely lost its head and forgotten its original objects
in an insane clamor for poetic anarchy.

CHAPTER VIII

THE REVOLUTION IN PROSE STYLE

"Literature is interpretation of life through the medium of language: it is language that makes manifest every effort and impression the writer wishes to arouse and kindle, and the problem of language, of the use of the medium in all its aspects, is the basic problem of every work of literature."
—ELIZABETH A. DREW, "The Modern Novel."

G REAT as have been the recent innovations in poetic form, they are scarcely more pronounced than the transformations in prose style. Since prose is normally a looser and less definitely chiseled medium than poetry, it is a trifle more difficult to detect and demonstrate the changes. But no follower of modern prose will doubt that the changes have been effected, and that our latest writers have adopted a style which differs sometimes subtly and sometimes palpably but almost always fundamentally from the style of their predecessors. And, as in the case of poetry, the movement has been in the direction of a greater freedom, a relaxing of rules and standards, a contempt for the old and a thirst for the unique, an untrammeled individualism and a general anarchy.

This is not to say, of course, that all our prose writers

have been in the vanguard of the revolution in style, any more than all our poets have been echoing the battle cries of the Imagists.   Yet our authors have enlisted in sufficient numbers to give the revolt something more than the aspect of a casual insurrection; and the rebels have not only invaded the enemy's territory but have captured his Capital, which means that they have set up a government of their own and are now the center of authority to which all our younger writers must look.   And the mandates they issue are many and imperious, but the chief of these is that no mandate shall be obeyed.

For the lawlessness governing the modern prose style is paralleled only by the lawlessness of *vers libre;* and its disregard of form is unrivaled outside of the realm of free verse.   By this I do not intend reference to the shapelessness of whole novels and plays, which I have already mentioned; I am speaking of the amorphous qualities of those smaller units of composition, the phrase, the sentence and the paragraph, which are the bricks out of which our writers must build their works of art.   It would seem superfluous to state that such bricks should be of a size and shape adapted to their particular use, and should not be piled up without regard to the total effect they are designed to produce. But this fact is precisely what many of the modernists seem to overlook, and in the treatment of their material they suggest architects who plan the second story of a building without reference to the style or construction of the first or the third.

There has grown up, indeed, an actual contempt for what would once have been considered the refinements of style. Such elements as symmetry and balance, smoothness and polish, are generally despised as somehow effeminate and unworthy. Instead, the idea of a blustering virility appears to have won preëminence; there seems to be a widespread belief that whatever is rough-hewn and crude is therefore impressive and strong. As a result, crudity of style has come to be valued, while ease, grace and magnificence are regarded almost as marks of degeneracy. Thus, one could hardly stigmatize a present-day author more severely than to say that he writes in the "grand manner"; while one could scarcely give him higher praise than to state that he uses the dialect of a "hairy-chested he-man" and that his work reeks of the "red loam."

As an example of that "grand manner" which has fallen into disrepute, let me quote the following, for which Ruskin is responsible:

"In the edifices of Man there should be such reverent worship and following, not only of the spirit which rounds the pillars of the forest, and arches the vault of the avenue—which gives veining to the leaf, and polish to the shell, and grace to every pulse that animates animal organization,—but of that also which reproves the pillars of the earth, and builds up her barren precipices into the coldness of the clouds, and lifts her shadowy cones of mountain purple into the pale arch of the sky; for these, and other glories more than these, refuse not to connect themselves in his thoughts, with the work of his own hand; the gray cliff loses not its nobleness when it reminds us of some Cyclopean waste of mural stone; the pin-

nacles of the rocky promontory arrange themselves, unde-graded, into fantastic semblances of fortress towers; and even the awful cone of the far-off mountain has a melancholy mixed with that of its own solitude, which is cast from the images of nameless tumuli on white sea-shores, and of heaps of reedy clay, into which chambered cities melt in their mortality."

No doubt this passage is somewhat consciously majestic in phraseology, and no doubt it is rhetorical—but is it any more offensive to be rhetorical than, let us say, to be grammatical, since what is rhetoric but a device for making expression more effective? Rhetoric can be objectionable only when it becomes too obvious and artificial; but, even though there be some artificiality in the above paragraph, the rhythm of its periods and the magnificence of its phrases are more than ample compensation.

Yet in the eyes of the modernist they would be no compensation at all. No present-day author would be forgiven for resorting to such a style; and a writer discussing the "edifices of man" would be expected to proceed somewhat in the manner of Edna Ferber, in the following passage from *So Big:*

"Dirk was wretched. He pointed out objects of interest to General Goguet. Sixty miles of boulevard. Park system. Finest in the country. Grand Boulevard. Drexel Boulevard. Jackson Park. Illinois Central Trains. Terrible, yes, but they were electrifying. Going to make 'em run by electricity, you know. Things wouldn't look so dirty after that. Halsted Street. Longest street in the world."

Possibly it will be pointed out that Miss Ferber's method is adequate for her purpose, and that there is no similarity between that purpose and Ruskin's. And both these points may be conceded without dispute—but a comparison of the two passages will serve to illustrate the difference between the stately style that has fallen into disfavor and the simple or "natural" style that has replaced it.

But before tracing further the stylistic contrasts between the earlier authors and the new and describing the various modern schools of prose, it may be well to say a word regarding the general principles of style. Why all this concern about the garments in which our writing is dressed? Why is the mere wording considered important so long as our ideas are somehow communicated? Are we not after all troubling ourselves about the pettiest of externals, and is the polish worth the effort of polishing, the graceful completed product superior to its rough-hewn prototype? So the modern scorner of style would ask—and his questions must be answered seriously before we can judge contemporary work.

To begin with, we may admit that style, like all the other agencies of literary creation, may at times be abused, and that an occasional writer may give it an attention it does not deserve, and may devote a disproportionate amount of care to a few glittering and well rounded externals. But this does not at all affect the main issue. It does not affect the fact that style is the most important instrument of literary expression;

that it is an artistic tool shaped by the writer's personality, and the only means of giving the personality scope in words; and that one can no more avoid style than one can avoid the use of the alphabet, although, if one's style be poor, one's achievement will be correspondingly limited.

The best style may be described as that which most truly, lucidly and appropriately expresses the contents of the communicating mind,—truly, because the first aim of any writing is to reveal with accuracy that which the writer thinks and feels,—lucidly, because it is the author's duty to remove all possible impediments in the way of his ideas,—and appropriately, because every detail should be appareled in that phraseology which accords best with its inherent nature.

It is about the question of appropriateness that most of the disagreements regarding style will revolve. Few critics will deny that an author's style should represent his thoughts with clarity and exactitude, and few will contend that it should not be appropriate—but how many will be in accord as to just what is fitting? For example, if a writer's topic be a horse race or a baseball game, is it not proper for him to express himself in slang? and if his subject be the banging of subway cars and the jangling of street traffic, is it not becoming to write with that lack of smoothness and harmony characteristic of subways and crowded streets?

No doubt there will be many to concede such liberties, and I would not be one of those to deny them. But it seems to me that the theme should dominate the

expression,—if a man choose a dignified subject, then
his style is unsuitable unless it is dignified; and if he
select a beautiful subject, then his style is not appropriate unless it is beautiful. Of course, if the subject
be complicated and involved, the style need not also be
involved (though in most cases it would be); and if the
subject be obscure, the style would not be improved by
obscurity.

But while a loose, rude or even disjointed style may
be appropriate in some cases, I believe that such a
style is never to be found in the best literature—and for
the reason that the subject of the best literature never
demands such a style. Rather, what is required, in
addition to lucidity and accuracy, is a perfect symmetry
and coördination, an harmonious blending of part with
part, a careful weeding out of all discordant elements
and a smoothness and ease of composition which produces what we may term "the style that conceals style."
On the more technical side, a good prose style should
have a definite rhythm, more varied than the rhythm
of poetry and yet not wholly different; and this should
never be obvious but should constitute a sort of underlying pattern, since for some half-explained reason
the human mind seems to turn unconsciously to rhythm
in its moments of ecstasy or exaltation, and words and
phrases which are jarring and non-rhythmical tend to
break the mood and shatter the illusion.

In making these remarks, I am far from wishing
to lay down explicit rules—it is merely my opinion that
there are unwritten rules which writers must follow

subconsciously if their work is to be effective. Let the completed product contain incongruities of style; let part not harmonize fully with part; let the marks of the author's battle with his material still be apparent, or let the writing have an abruptness that breaks the continuity and jolts and disturbs the subjective mind—and the book will in all probability be short-lived and inconsequential. No matter how vital and potentially impressive the material, it will have little chance of surviving the handicap of an inappropriate style; and even if it does survive it will possess but a fraction of its possible appeal. This is because, while style is really no more than the means to an end, it is the agency without which the end cannot be reached, the road that must be skillfully traveled on the way to any important goal.

Having now examined a few of the fundamentals, let us turn to present-day tendencies, and seek to determine how far our authors have progressed in their mastery of style.

Perhaps the most notable of recent developments is what may be termed the "back to nature" movement in style. Just as the free versifiers have claimed to seek a return to the "rhythm of natural breathing," so the modern prose writers have been pleading on behalf of the "rhythm of natural speech." They have sought to escape from our hyper-civilized literary atmosphere, to cast off the suffocating and conventional garments of rhetoric, and to plunge into the backwoods in a state of primitive nudity and freedom. The artifices of the

sophisticated shall enchain them no longer; no longer
shall they grow effeminate amid the luxuriance of words
and phrases; they shall make of themselves what they
were intended to be, and shall enact the rôles of Adam
and Eve in a literary Garden of Eden. Not the super-
refined elegance of the erudite but the unspoiled vigor
of the savage shall be their ideal and goal; they aim
to give back to literature that primeval power it possessed before it succumbed to the stilted diction of our
Carlyles and our De Quinceys. And the method they
favor is one that would cast all the laces, wall hang-
ings and filigrees of art into the refuse heap and substitute the ungarnished robustness of the log cabin.

All this may be very well—provided that it is
founded on a sound theory. But is it founded on a
sound theory? Is there anything natural about literature, and can there ever be anything natural? Is not
the very use of words an artificiality, a necessarily imperfect contrivance to facilitate the transmission of
ideas? And is not the employment of the written word
an artificiality built upon an artificiality, the utilization
of a code of visible symbols to represent other symbols
which are only audible? Then how expect to establish
a natural style?—unless by means of a wordless mental
telepathy? Does not the history of literature show us
that with each new development of thought and each
new complexity of emotion, we have drifted further
from a style that might be conceived to be natural?
And when we say "natural" do we not really mean
"elementary"? Are not most of the so-called natural

styles those that deal in elementary thoughts and feelings?

At all events, I for one suspect that naturalness and shallowness are frequently synonymous. From a perusal of many books by members of the "back to nature" school, I am led to conclude that the works termed natural are often the ones most deficient in intellectual and emotional content. As in the case of so many inferior compositions, the style may be appropriate for the subject matter—but the subject matter is apt to be trivial and slight.

In order to illustrate this fact, let me offer one or two examples from recent fiction. And, to begin with, let us confine our attention to that branch of the "back to nature" school which may be known as the Conversational Division, since its devotees attempt to model their style upon normal conversation. Here, for instance, is a typical passage from a short story by Ring Lardner:

> "Mother says that when I start talking I never know when to stop. But I tell her the only time I get a chance is when she ain't around, so I have to make the most of it. I guess the fact is neither one of us would be welcome in a Quaker meeting, but as I tell Mother, what did God give us tongues for if He didn't want we should use them? Only she says He didn't give them to us to say the same thing over and over, like I do, and repeat myself."

It is not my contention that the style of this selection does not accord with the author's purpose; it is only that the purpose requiring such a style can admit of no depth, intensity or subtlety of content. And the same may be said of the following, by Jerome K. Jerome:

"I am not a good fisherman myself. I devoted a considerable amount of attention to the subject at one time, and was getting on, as I thought, fairly well; but the old hands told me that I should never be any real good at it, and advised me to give it up . . . they were sure I should never make anything of a fisherman. I had not got sufficient imagination."

In both the above passages the style of the work corresponds with the spirit, since it is the author's intention to produce the impression of actual conversation. But as much cannot be said of certain other modern narratives—narratives in which there is a conversational style and yet no reason for creating a conversational effect.

Consider, for example, the way in which a certain present-day British writer begins his story:

"This isn't a story. It's an attempt at reconstruction. Given my knowledge of the principals—Mary Jarvis and her mother, Mrs. St. Luth—I think I can do it.

"Mary Jarvis was my mother, and Mrs. St. Luth, of course, my grandmother. Thank God, I'm a modern and can look at them impersonally—judge each on her own merits, as it were.

"My mother and my grandmother made scenes as other women make jumpers. It was their form of self-expression. . . ."

Here the author is attempting a tale which differs in no essential from other tales told by an onlooker—and all stories must be told by an onlooker, either actual or imaginary. Then why must this be given the rude and idiomatic impress of conversation, while other works in a similar vein are constructed with an attempt at literary finish? It appears to me that the author, in his endeavor to be simple and natural, has fallen victim to a common fallacy: he has assumed that the phraseology normal in oral expression is also normal on the printed page. And this, I believe, implies a fundamental misconception of the nature and purpose of writing: it involves the confusion of supposing that to write is basically the same as to speak.

Actually, however, both the source and the object of vocal and written expression are utterly different: in the one case the words flow spontaneously, and without any artistic arrangement or restraint, and are directed ordinarily to an individual or small group of individuals; in the other case the words must be meditated, they must be chosen and coördinated according to artistic tenets, and they are aimed at a broad unseen audience whose numbers cannot be estimated. And is it natural to address the great assemblage as one would address a small circle of one's acquaintances? Would it be natural, let us say, for the orator to speak in the packed lecture hall as he would speak in private to his intimates? Then how much less natural to appear before a huge invisible gathering as though one were seated in one's own room alone with some chosen friend? Must we not conclude, rather, that the term "natural" is only relative, and that what is perfectly normal and appropriate on some occasions would be strained and affected on others: so that it may be as artificial to write in an informal style as to converse with rhetorical formality? It would seem to me, indeed, that since literature is a highly specialized medium, it has highly specialized requirements, and has need for a vocabulary and technique which cannot correspond with the vocabulary and technique of ordinary speech for the reason that its methods and purposes are not the same.

But is not simplicity to be desired? the reader will ask. By all means! It is even to be demanded when the theme makes it possible without loss. Yet a simple style need not necessarily be conversational; and, however unstrained and natural it seems, it must be definitely subject to artistic law and to methods that are not the methods of verbal utterance.

In the following passage by James Stephens, for example, we find a simple and becoming style—but by no stretching of definition could it be termed a conversational style:

"Day after day she sat by Ailill's bed, and the beam of love that she had shown to him was always in her eyes, and the hand that had been gentle in his was never withdrawn from his hand that sought it.

"But she did not speak much.

"It seemed to her that words were difficult or unnecessary things: nor could she remember many of them; and those that she could remember did not seem appropriate.

"For at times, as from a void, words would arise, unbidden, unsought . . ."

The same remarks apply to the following, from Lord Dunsany's *The Sword and the Idol*, although in this case, to be sure, the theme is far from that of ordinary conversation:

"It was a cold winter's evening late in the Stone Age; the sun had gone down blazing over the plains of Thold; there were no clouds, only the chill blue sky and the immanence of stars; and the surface of the sleeping Earth began to harden against the cold of the night. . . . Suddenly there became manifest in the midst of the plain that fearful portent of the presence of Man—a little flickering fire. And the children of Earth who prowl abroad by night looked sideways at it and snarled and edged away; all but the wolves, who came a little nearer, for it was winter, and the wolves were hungry, and they had come in thousands from the mountains, and they said in their hearts, 'We are strong.' "

As opposed to the orderly and fluent rhythms of the above, many members of the "back to nature" school have adopted a style that may be termed the "dot and dash" or "staccato," since it is characterized by the jolting abruptness of a telegraphic message, and short words and short sentences are its outstanding features. Sometimes these "dot and dash" writers identify themselves with the conversational group, sometimes they are content to form a group of their own; but, in any case, they seem to agree with their conversational brethren in aiming for simplicity, directness and "naturalness" of style.

An example of their work is to be found in the excerpt from Edna Ferber, which we quoted several pages back; another is the following, from D. H. Lawrence's *Sons and Lovers:*

"He got to the cottage at about eleven o'clock. Miriam was busy preparing dinner. She looked so perfectly in keeping with the little kitchen, ruddy and busy. He kissed her and sat down to watch. The room was small and cosy. The sofa was covered all over with a sort of linen in squares of red and pale blue, old, much washed, but pretty. There was a stuffed owl in a case over a corner cupboard. The sunlight came through the leaves of the scented geraniums in the window. She was cooking a chicken in his honor. It was their cottage for the day, and they were man and wife. He beat the eggs for her and peeled the potatoes."

It is needless to comment upon the chaotic, illogical effect produced by such a passage; upon the incoherence of the paragraph, and the lack of a natural sequence; upon the fact that the abrupt, jerky sentences emphasize things of unequal importance as of equal weight, and lead us to feel less interest, for instance, in the circumstance that the hero and heroine "were man and wife" than that "he beat the eggs for her and peeled the potatoes."

It may be conceded that an occasional paragraph may gain by a staccato style; but when such a style is prolonged to the length of an entire book (and there are many contemporary volumes composed in such a style) the total effect is intolerably monotonous and tiresome.

Even though short sentences may occasionally be highly effective, they are usually the mark either of elementary thoughts and feelings or else of thoughts and feelings unnaturally subdivided.   In its essence, a sentence may be regarded as the expression of a completed idea; if the idea be simple and without complication, it may, of course, be embodied in a very few words; but if it be wide-ranging and intricate it may properly extend over many lines.   Thus, we will find that children ordinarily express themselves in brief and disjointed sentences; while those of philosophic bent are likely to build up sentences longer than the average paragraph, and, moreover, to make each sentence flow logically into the next.   In the one case, we have the mark of the simple and undeveloped mind; in the other, the impress of the complex and mature intellect.   It is possible, indeed, to divide a long sentence into several short ones by the simple process of a change in punctuation; but the inevitable result will be an effect of discontinuity, a blurring of logical boundaries, and a readjustment of emphasis until what is small is in danger of appearing great and what is great is in danger of seeming small.   In the typical staccato style, all statements receive virtually equal emphasis, and there is little opportunity for that shading and coloring which is the mark of an advanced perceptiveness; and thus we find either that confusion of values which is evident in the passage from *Sons and Lovers,* or else that cataloguing of elementary impressions which we observed in the quotation from *So Big.*

And there is no alternative: the staccato style, when resorted to at all, is either used inappropriately in place of a better knitted and more fluent style, or else is appropriately employed to express sentiments and thoughts which lack complexity and, therefore, are those of the child or the savage or of a person temporarily reduced to the state of the child or the savage by an emotional or mental crisis.

This is equally true when the staccato style is adopted in order to produce an impressionistic or "Imagistic" effect. Let us examine, for example, an excerpt from Ben Hecht's novel, *Eric Dorn:*

"Long days. Short days. Outside the window was an ant-hill street. And an ant-hill of days. In the stores they were already selling calendars for the next year. Outside the window was a flat roof. By looking at the flat roof you remembered that Mary James was married. Unexpectedly. You came out of the ant-hill street, climbed the stairs, and sat down and looked at the flat roof. Long days, short days turned themselves over on the flat roof, and turned themselves over in your heart.

"Occasionally an event. Events were things that differed from putting on your shoes or buying butter in the grocery store. There was an event now. It challenged the importance of the flat roof. Hazlitt was sitting in the room and talking. Rachel listened.

"An eloquent event. But words jumbled into sound. Loud sounds. Soft sounds . . ."

It will be evident at a glance that this passage contains no thought not of a primitive nature—no thought that might not be harbored by the most rudimentary of minds, a mind incapable of reasoning, of forming conclusions or correlating events, or of undertaking any of those logical processes incidental to the act of putting two and two together. A person whose most involved and subtle reflection was "loud sounds" or "soft sounds" would of course make a separate sentence of "loud sounds" or "soft sounds"—and the fact that the author intended an impressionistic effect does not in the least modify this consideration, since what is impressionism but a dealing in elementary impressions?

And the relative ineffectiveness of the method may best be shown by a simple comparison. No doubt Mr. Hecht desired to produce a mood of dreary monotony, a mood that might indicate how dingy and flat and meaningless was life; but does his oppressive atmosphere really oppress one in anything like the same degree as that summoned forth on sundry occasions by a certain of his predecessors, one Edgar Allan Poe?

Here, for example, is the beginning of *The Fall of the House of Usher*—and it may be noted that Poe writes in long sentences, without any inclination toward the "dot and dash" method, and without any straining to be simple, direct or natural:

"During the whole of a dull, dark, and soundless day in the autumn of the year, when the clouds hung oppressively low in the heavens, I had been passing alone, on horseback, through a singularly dreary tract of country; and at length found myself, as the shades of evening drew on, within view of the melancholy House of Usher. I know not how it was; but, with the first glimpse of the building, a sense of insufferable gloom pervaded my spirit. I say insufferable; for the feeling was unrelieved by any of that half-pleasurable, because poetic, sentiment, with which the mind usually receives even the sternest natural images of the desolate or terrible.

I looked upon the scene before me—upon the mere house, and the simple landscape features of the domain—upon the bleak walls—upon the vacant eye-like windows—upon a few rank sedges—and upon a few white trunks of decayed trees—with an utter depression of soul which I can compare to no earthly sensation more properly than to the after-dream of the reveler upon opium—the bitter lapse into every-day life—the hideous dropping off of the veil. . . ."

There may be some who profess to find the verbiage of this passage forced and artificial; yet, even though Poe's manner of expression be falling into disrepute, it appears to me that his most august phrases are natural and unaffected by the side of Mr. Hecht's seeming simplicity.

Would Poe have improved the naturalness of his work, for example, if he had written as follows, in the modern style?——

A dull day. A dark day. A soundless day. It was autumn. The clouds hung oppressively low. I had been passing alone, on horseback, through a dreary tract of country. Toward sunset, I found myself approaching the melancholy House of Usher. A dull day. A dark day. A soundless day. I don't know how it was, but as soon as I saw the building I became frightfully sad. I say frightfully, because, honestly, there was nothing at all to relieve my mind. I looked upon the scene before me. There was the mere house. The simple landscape. The bleak walls. The vacant eye-like windows. A few rank sedges. A few white trunks of trees. I felt for all the world like a dope-fiend just coming to. A dull day. A dark day. A soundless day.

According to modern theories and practice, this is a more natural style than that actually employed by Poe.   Yet is it likely that, if Poe had written in such a manner, we would still be reading *The Fall of the House of Usher?*

In what way, then, is Poe's work superior to that of his more modern successor?   In the case of the earlier story, one feels that the author is writing out of the compulsion of a deeply felt mood; in the case of *Eric Dorn,* one is fairly certain that the narrator has at least one eye on his prospective audience and that he is not undesirous of winning his laurels for cleverness.

And this is but typical of a whole group of writers— writers in whom the desire to be considered "smart" is apparently the outstanding motive.   Perhaps the last consideration is the truth of their statements, and next to the last is the intensity with which those statements are felt—the first necessity is to be "different" and to produce a glittering effect.   And, singularly enough, there is very little real cleverness among all these glib young writers.   There is much straining after gaudy and bizarre effects; there is much ingenious word manipulation, and a general atmosphere of egotism and supersophistication; there is a blatant and too-conscious questing for originality, regardless of the fact that true originality mocks at the seeker and emanates unbidden from the distinctive personality.   And the total effect of all this striving for uniqueness is that of a vaudeville show produced by amateurs. The wording of the piece is a little obvious and a little crude; the acting is a trifle maladroit and more than a trifle overdone—apparently each member of the cast wishes to be considered the central luminary. The result is that most of them are dull luminaries indeed. Occasionally, it must be admitted, a performer of genuine cleverness does appear—a Bernard Shaw, a Stephen Leacock, a James Branch Cabell—but these are so rare and so exceptional as merely to make the others seem all the pettier by comparison. Yet meanwhile these others put forth herculean efforts; they strain their voices valiantly to declaim about their "indigo indignities" or about "the poised lyric of the sky"; and because they make up in numbers for what they lack in genuineness, they have established an important rival of the "back to nature" school, which may be termed the "paint and powder" school, since its chief object seems to be to put powder and paint on nature and to spread gilt and tinsel over the arch of the rainbow and the cheek of the rose.

It must be admitted, however, that the boundaries of the "paint and powder" school are not rigidly defined; frequently they overlap those of a larger and still more important school, the school of Confusion and Chaos.

This faction is one that cannot be overlooked in any discussion of present-day style. Its members are legion, and range from the lowest level of obscurity to the highest pitch of fame; their methods are curious and widely varied, and are distinguished by anything from a common disregard of logic to a chronic obtuseness of vision. Some are members of the Confusion group by choice, some by necessity, some by carelessness, and some by virtue of their shortness of sight; some have a congenital preference for dark places, and a few would have no chance for distinction were they to be seen in the light; but a majority would indignantly deny their allegiance, for it is a peculiar quality of Confusion and Chaos that those who are governed by them are least conscious of their rule.

To find examples of the influences of these divinities is no difficult matter; indeed, it would be no easy matter to avoid finding examples. Therefore let us try to show a few of the devious ways in which Confusion and Chaos operate. Let us begin with some of their simpler manifestations; let us seek to illustrate their method of blurring an idea by the common process of Irrelevant Additions—a process that would permit one to bring a discussion of the nebula hypothesis into a paragraph dealing with the Volstead Act, or a commentary on marriage customs in China into a demonstration of one of Euclid's theorems.

In the following passage, from *South Wind,* Norman Douglas does not go quite so far as the method permits, but he goes far enough to exemplify a common tendency:

"The bishop was feeling rather sea-sick. Confoundedly sea-sick, in fact.

"This annoyed him. For he disapproved of sickness in

every shape and form. His own state of body was far from
satisfactory at that moment; Africa—he was Bishop of Bam-
popo in the Equatorial Regions—had played the devil with
his lower gastric department and made him almost an in-
valid; a circumstance of which he was nowise proud, seeing
that ill-health led to inefficiency in all walks of life. There
was nothing he despised more than inefficiency. Well or
ill, he always insisted on getting through his tasks in a
business-like fashion. That was the way to live, he used
to say. Get through with it. Be perfect of your kind, whatever that kind may be. Hence his sneaking fondness for
the natives—they were such fine, healthy animals."

It would be superfluous to observe that the author
here displays a not unusual propensity to go rambling
all over the universe—and that his manner of rambling
is one of enormous leaps and jumps. Nor for two con-
secutive instants is the reader's attention focused upon
any one subject—first it is sea-sickness; then it is the
Bishop's general health; then his official position in
Africa, then his opinions on inefficiency and a summary
of his philosophy of life, and finally the physical condi-
tion of the natives. How, I wonder, does the author
expect the reader to derive any single and definite impression from so jumbled a passage?

Examples of this same discursive style, this same
lack of logical coherence, might be found in the works
of perhaps half the writers of the day. But the above
illustration will suffice for our purposes, particularly
since a mere blurring of effect constitutes one of the
slightest misdemeanors of the school of Confusion and
Chaos.

The offense becomes much more objectionable when the author not only overloads his paragraph with irrelevant detail, but so overcharges his sentences that the reader has difficulty in arriving at his meaning. Consider, for example, the way in which Irvin S. Cobb begins one of his short stories:

"When Judge Priest, on this particular morning, came puffing into his chambers at the courthouse, looking, in his broad beam and in his costume of flappy, loose white ducks, a good deal like an old-fashioned full-rigger with all sails set, his black shadow, Jeff Poindexter, had already finished the job of putting the quarters to rights for the day."

By means of painstaking study, it is not impossible to determine precisely what the author meant—but why need he have left it for the reader to arrange and coördinate the material? and why need he have weakened his effect by providing half a dozen separate foci of attention? Mr. Cobb has obviously tried to tell us everything in a single breath; and as a result it is difficult for the reader to concentrate upon any one point, and the total effect left by the sentence is a blur.

Much the same may be said of the following, by Fannie Hurst:

"Where St. Louis begins to peter out into brick-and-limestone kilns and great scars of unworked and overworked quarries, the first and more pretentious of its suburbs take up —Benson, Maplehurst and Ridgewood Heights intervening with one-story brick cottages and two-story packing cases—

between the smoke of the city and the carefully parked Queen Anne quietude of Glenwood and Croton Grove."

But if this be not easy to follow, it is simplicity itself beside a sentence which I find in a certain recent volume of literary criticism:

"To this assumption—to me the conditions of all literary feeling and valuation—that kind of objective poetry, Milton's, in particular, in which verbal magnificence—magniloquence —surpasses all other qualities, is a difficult problem."

Certainly, the difficult problem in this case is for the reader to solve.

But not less puzzling is the riddle presented by certain advanced members of the school of Confusion and Chaos, who write in such a way that the reader may interpret them as suits his inclination. As an example, let us examine this sentence, from a story by T. F. Powys:

"Mr. Day, the pastor, always believed that if Mrs. Moggs could be persuaded to leave her little shop, that was also the village post office, upon a Sunday or any holiday, and go down and look at the sea, her soul's salvation would be sure to follow such a visit."

Are we to believe that Mr. Day wished Mrs. Moggs to leave her shop upon a Sunday or any holiday? or that the shop was the village post office upon a Sunday or any holiday? If the author means the former, he writes so as to imply that he means the latter. And, no

matter what he means, there is no excuse for distract-
ing the reader's attention by such ambiguity.

But the confusion in this case is negligible by comparison with that which one comes across time after
time in the works of a much better known writer—
Theodore Dreiser. The style of this novelist indicates
no more than an elementary effort to avoid a general
murkiness of effect; it exhibits a thorough devotion to
the creed of Confusion and Chaos. It would be possible to fill whole pages with quotations from Mr.
Dreiser alone; but a single example should suffice to
prove the point. The following is from *An American
Tragedy:*

> "Unfortunately, however, the Christmas dinner at the
> Griffiths, which included the Starks and their daughter Ara-
> bella, Mr. and Mrs. Wynant, who in the absence of their
> daughter Constance with Gilbert were dining with the Grif-
> fiths, the Arnolds, Anthonys, Harriets, Taylors and others of
> note in Lycurgus, so impressed and even overawed Clyde that
> although five o'clock came and then six, he was incapable
> of breaking away or thinking clearly and compellingly of his
> obligation to Roberta."

After reading this sentence, one is inclined to wonder
whether Clyde was the only one who was incapable of
"thinking clearly and compellingly." If Mr. Dreiser
had gone out of his way to provide examples of miscellaneous obscurities of style, he could hardly have
succeeded more perfectly than in this passage. We
may overlook the fact that the sentence is as overbur-

dened and topheavy as could be, for it has other and
even more amazing features. I feel sure, for example,
that the author did not mean us to believe that the
Starks' daughter Arabella was "Mr. and Mrs. Wy-
nant"; nor that the Griffiths were so cannibalistically
inclined as to include the Starks in their Christmas
dinner. Yet, if one does not reach such conclusions,
the fault is not Mr. Dreiser's.

And this sentence, it must be remembered, was not
culled from the class exercise of a High School sopho-
more—it represents the work of one of America's most
eminent and most experienced literary craftsmen.
Whether or not Mr. Dreiser could have done better
is beside the point; the fact that he has done so poorly
is all that counts. And if we had only one writer such
as he, and that writer had won only one quarter of his
recognition and turned out chaotic sentences with one
tenth his frequency, that fact alone would be sufficient
to indicate that lucidity of style was retreating along
with truth and appropriateness to the limbo of the
outworn and the neglected.

CHAPTER IX

SOME DOGMAS OF THE MODERNISTS

Neglect the rules each verbal critic lays,
For not to know some trifles, is a praise.
Most critics, fond of some subservient art,
Still make the whole depend upon a part.
　　　　—POPE, "An Essay on Criticism."

MOST revolutions, great or small, tend to move
not in a straight line but in a circle. Even
though launched amid a blaze of success and
thoroughly efficient in substituting the new order for
the old, they are likely to travel in wide curves that
bend back toward their starting place; and the current of reaction is likely to obscure or sweep away the
innovations, obliterating them in spirit if not in form.
Perhaps it is that the mind of man, being naturally
inelastic, cannot stretch itself far beyond the boundaries of the known and the familiar, but is subject
to a process of self-deception that makes it return to
old methods and old tenets even though it retains the
illusion of novelty. At all events, most of the revolutions in politics, thought and religion have ended in
more of an apparent than an actual change: the Pil-
grims revolted against intolerance in the Old World,

and substituted intolerance in the New; the system of Equity was instituted to offset the rigid English Common Law, and became as precedent-ridden and unyielding as the Common Law itself; the Revolution in Russia was aimed against an intolerable class tyranny, which it destroyed only in order to establish a class tyranny of an opposing type.

And so it is with revolutions in literature. However devastating and final the changes they are intended to inaugurate, it cannot be long before the arrows shot into the air will begin to turn again toward the earth. For a moment, when the darts are careering gayly skyward, it may be thought that a shaft is about to be launched into the sun or the moon; and for a long while some may actually retain the impression that the sun or the moon is their target; but more perspicacious observers will be convinced that the rebels are engaged in a vain contest with the laws of gravity, and that the upper empyrean will remain unaffected by all their efforts. The utmost that they will succeed in doing will be to drive other bowmen from the field and to call attention to themselves; but, unless they be indeed superhuman, they will be not altogether superior to those they have replaced, and their methods will bear more than a superficial resemblance to the methods of their predecessors.

In the case of the present literary revolution, one will find that the arrows are already falling to earth. The attack has been made, the missiles have come to a not unnatural futile ending; and while there has been a change in literary leadership, there have been many things that have altered in appearance only. And in a score of ways the old régime is still with us—although under another name. The revolt against old abuses has been consummated—but the abuses remain, although decked in slightly different garments. Thus, the chief objects of assault have been the conventions and the standardized machinery of the displaced group; but these have been quickly supplanted by new standardized machinery and new conventions. Consistency, alas! is as little the attribute of the literary revolutionists as of revolutionists in general; and they have proved themselves thoroughly human and entirely illogical by substituting a creed of their own for the creed they have overthrown, and by going so far in their zest to be free as to deny freedom to all who worship at different altars.

It requires but superficial observation to convince one that the literary revolution is approaching its final stages. It has reached the point of relative stability and of intolerance; it has grown systematic in its methods, and arrogant toward opposition; it has become stereotyped in its revolt against the stereotyped. Like a religion entrenched upon the stronghold of a fallen predecessor, it has issued its mandates and formulated its dogmas; and its high priests watch jealously to see that those dogmas are obeyed and that the offenders are penalized with literary excommunication.

But precisely what are the dogmas of the modernists?

They are many and rigid, and a majority of them should be evident from our previous discussion. But we have not been able to examine them all, and it may repay us to inquire in detail into a few of the more significant.

Paradoxically enough, one of the most insistent of modern dogmas is that which opposes the dogmatic. All that is platitudinous in thought or expression is anathema to the rebels (and who would dispute with them on this point?). But the rules of their revolt are so rigid that their very objections appear platitudinous; and in their disdain of the banal and the threadbare they go to such extremes that the threadbare seems refreshing by comparison. We have already spoken of that straining for effect which marks so much of modern literature; but we have not described the ludicrous extent to which that straining has been carried, nor how in many cases it represents but obedience to that dogma which requires the writer to be "different" and "original." There is no term of contempt that the modernists use to more searing effect than the word "cliché"; yet this very expression, as Alfred Noyes has pointed out in *Some Aspects of Modern Poetry*, has itself become a cliché; and our writers are woefully convention-bound in their struggles to escape the shadow of this dread epithet.

Thus, for example, it is a well established fact, authenticated by centuries of observation, that the normal color of the sky is blue; but for the modernist to call the sky blue would be to perpetrate a cliché, since men both poetically inclined and prosaic have long been disposed to speak of "blue skies."   Whether the innovators would consider it more appropriate to call the sky "pink" or "lavender" or "purple" is more than I can say, for I cannot pretend to be initiated into the profounder mysteries; but at least I can testify that "blue skies" have become unmentionable, along with barbarisms such as "green fields," "yellowing woods" and "red sunsets."   Instead, since these are days of rarer colors, we have one of our poets speaking of "topaz phrases" and another depicting the spirit of the sea and clouds as of a "pistache" hue.

From my own point of view—and I readily admit that I am prejudiced in this, as in most other matters—I cannot see the object of avoiding the hackneyed in pursuance of hackneyed rules, nor in being original according to prescription.   It would seem to me that to say that one must never employ the phrase "green grass" or "fragrant flowers" is as arbitrary as to say that one must never avoid them—a law of negatives may be quite as rigid as a law of positives, and there can be but little gain in the substitution of the former for the latter.   And what have our revolutionists done except to offer a negative convention in the place of a more positive one?   If I am not permitted to do certain things, am I any freer than if I am compelled to do them?   And am I any less the slave to a dictatorial tradition?   The point of emphasis has merely been shifted; the sphere has revolved halfway on its axis; what was above is now beneath, and what was beneath is now above; but in essence there has been no change. And so I believe that the modernists, in rebelling against the dogmatic, have merely followed the time-honored course of insurgents in most fields, and have exalted dogmas of their own making upon the ruins of the dogmas they have supplanted.

None the less, I do not mean to deny that they have accomplished a certain amount of good in discarding the strait-jacket of old conventions, and in aiming toward directness, freshness and crispness of expression. The trouble, as I have already indicated, is that they have swung the pendulum so far to the opposite extreme as to counteract most of their gains; in place of the hackneyed they have furnished something so labored and forced as almost to supply an argument for that which they oppose. I for one will admit, for example, that phrases such as "soft snow" or "gentle snow" are commonplace; yet I vastly prefer them to the more original "spider snow" of a modern, for, after all, the snow may at times be soft and gentle, but is it ever in the least like the dark-bodied prowling little fly-catcher?

Again, when I find a modern poet writing of "the indelible persuasiveness of single forms" or of "the bold incoherence of love" or "the spontaneous redundancy of nature," I will acknowledge at once the author's claim to novelty, and yet I feel that "Baa, baa, black sheep, have you any wool?" makes better and more intelligible poetry. Likewise, I should much rather hear mention of the undeniably trite "rushing rivers" or "downy clouds" than to have "the moon's delicate tusk" compared to a goad (though this is probably the first reference in all literature to a delicate goad); and I should much sooner think of an overworked but apt "fiery passion" than to believe, with one of my contemporaries, that my ecstasy "has long blue fingers like the sea."

Singularly enough, the modern dogmas overlook that very naturalness which would seem to be their objective. Possibly their exponents have microscopes for eyes; they see small things very well, and great things not at all. And in their preoccupation with words and phrases, they forget that words and phrases are not the only objects of importance in a literary work—there is such a thing as a totality of effect, which may depend upon no distinction in details, but may be based upon the harmonious interweaving of part with part, without straining or jolting, without dislocation of any segment, without any distraction of attention to glittering minor facets or emphasis upon those portions which do not require to be emphatic. The reader will remember, for example, how well Wordsworth succeeds in passages such as the following:

> Three years she grew in sun and shower;
> Then Nature said, 'A lovelier flower
>   On earth was never sown;
> This child I to myself will take;
> She shall be mine, and I will make
>   A lady of my own.

'Myself will to my darling be
Both law and impulse: and with me
The girl, in rock and plain,
In earth and heaven, in glade and bower,
Shall feel an overseeing power
To kindle or restrain.'

"Lovelier flower," "law and impulse," "overseeing power"—what phrase is there here that is not utterly commonplace, utterly cliché? And yet the total effect is impressive! Is not this because Wordsworth has given more attention to the whole than to the part, because he desired to write a poem rather than a series of phrases?

But in the matter of verbal uniqueness and originality, he of course cannot compare with many of the moderns—does not compare, for instance, with Walter Conrad Arensberg, whose poem on "Ing" contains not one overworked expression:

Ing? Is it possible to mean ing?
Suppose
            for the termination in g
                                     a disoriented
                                     series
            of the simple fractures
                                     in sleep
                                     Sophorific
       Has accordingly a value for soap.

Poems of this type are perhaps the outcome of a second of the modern dogmas—the dogma that literature should progress. During the past few decades

the whole world seems to have gone mad with the idea
of progress; it seems to be the general notion that we
are climbing step by step up an endless staircase that
will lead us beyond the stars; and the belief appears
to be not only that we may ascend but that we must,
and that the advance must take place equally in all
fields of human endeavor. Probably this conception
owes its birth largely to the evolutionary doctrine in
biology; and no doubt it is through a false biological
analogy that we have come to believe that everything
human should go continuously forward. Even in
nature—if we make nature our final court of appeal—
there is no such thing as uninterrupted evolution.
Progress does indeed occur now and then, but only
when there is some advantage in readjustment; and
there are some species of animals—among the inverte-
brates in particular—which do not seem to have
changed essentially throughout many geologic ages.
While unlimited in ingenuity, nature would seem to be
a cautious innovator; she attempts changes only when
they seem to be desirable or necessary owing to an
altered environment; and if there is no need of adapta-
tion, and a race can endure in safety without organic
transformation, then in all probability no transformation will be begun. Were human progress to be mod-
eled upon progress in nature, it would occur only when
there was some maladjustment that needed to be re-
paired—and this is just when human progress is most
often in abeyance.

These remarks apply in particular to developments

in literature. In political, economic and social spheres, I will gladly concede, we are in need of rapid progress in order to overcome acute and specific evils. But I do not believe that there is any such necessity in literature, unless it be the necessity of advancing away from the advances of the past few years. For what is progress except a movement to remedy deficiencies, to substitute the perfect for the imperfect? And is not the idea of perpetual progress contradictory, since it implies the impossibility of reaching that mark which progress—by the very laws of its nature—is steadily approaching?

Now I will not contend that literature has altogether found its goal, or that it has as yet achieved perfection—but I do maintain that, as compared with the non-artistic fields of human endeavor, as compared with political science or sociology or law, it has reached heights that may be regarded as perfect. Have we ever invented any system of government, for example, that approaches as near to the ideal as *Hamlet* or *King Lear* approach to the ideal drama? Or has any legal code or scheme of labor or taxation ever fulfilled itself so well as Shelley's *West Wind* fulfills itself as a lyric? It requires only the most cursory glance to convince one that, although we are still on the lowlands of social development, we have mounted repeatedly to the highlands of art, and on one or two supreme occasions have scaled those peaks that mark the summit of the attainable world.

And yet, to listen to our literary radicals, one might imagine that artistic progress were relatively as essential as progress in the administration of justice or the distribution of wealth. One might fancy that there was no accomplishment behind us; that all the great achievements were ahead. And because the world will be in a sorry pass if we fail to effect some reform in our clumsy social machinery, we must believe that literature will perish unless we tinker with the smooth-working machinery of art.

It is not inconceivable, of course, that some improvement might be introduced in that machinery; that advantageous new methods and devices might be employed. But no such methods or devices have been contributed by our literary revolutionists. And, in any event, it is improbable that any rapid or fundamental change can be made by them or any one else; for our literature is the combined and tested product of innumerable writers and thinkers,—the foundations have been established so solidly that any alteration must necessarily be painstaking and slow. It may be that there are laws which would enable us to write sonnets more perfect than those of Keats, songs abler than ever issued from the pen of Burns, and ballads beside which *The Ancient Mariner* would seem colorless and weak; but such laws have never yet been discovered, and it is doubtful if they ever will be—and if they are indeed found, it will be not by tumultuous dynamiters of tradition, but by sober and thoughtful lovers of art.

But meanwhile we need not be discouraged if we gain no new miraculous keys to literary progress. We need not even despair if literature remains static and we explore no heights above those attained by Shakespeare, Virgil and Dante; we may go so far as to feel satisfied that our heritage—unlike the social heritage of our race—is a magnificent and even an inspiring one; and we may be content to scale again those peaks our predecessors have conquered, while in searching for new pinnacles we must take care not to forfeit our mastery over the old.

A third modern dogma—and one not less strongly entrenched than the dogma of progress—is that literature should be a revelation of life. And this dogma represents a limitation typical of the revolutionary doctrine: it repeats the old fallacy of treating a part as the whole, and defines life as that portion of existence which is subject to sense perception. In our chapter on modern realism we have already touched upon this matter, indicating the mistake of identifying reality with material reality; but some further clarification will perhaps be necessary.

To begin with, we may admit that literature should indeed be a revelation of life—but precisely what interpretation should we give to the term life? Should we conceive of it as do the horse and the cow?—should we think of the world as a simple and easily understandable place, lacking mystery and complication, with its meaning written on the surface?—and should we hold that the only things that happen are those we can see, hear or smell? If this be our view, our test of life will be the criterion of appearance, and we will logically be able to consider ourselves alive only so long as our senses are in action.

But it is to be doubted whether any, even the most literal of realists, take so circumscribed a view of life —no one fails wholly to recognize that man has thoughts and feelings, and that these form a part of life. Yet precisely how far does the recognition go? Unable as we are to overlook completely the subjective side of man, do we emphasize it at its true worth? Even if we be of the school of psychological realists, are we ready to acknowledge that everything affecting the psychology of man is part of life? When a writer draws his subject matter, for example, from festering tenements and from motor-laden streets, we will readily enough credit him with revealing life; but when he delves down into the profoundest caves of his being, and unbares fancies that have dazzled or harassed or bewildered him, is he dealing with life any the less than if he describes the flickering of his eyelashes or the color of his shoes? True, that which is life for him may find no parallel in the experience of most of his readers—but what two of us lead identical lives even in superficials? For him the things he has imagined and dreamt and longed for and suffered may have a deeper and more poignant reality than the things he sees and feels—therefore, in portraying life, he must necessarily be concerned with the things he has imagined and dreamt. And in many cases, I believe, these will create a more veracious picture than the most scrupulous and detailed listing of externals. So vague a poem as *Ulalume,* for instance, is probably a truer representation of the life of Poe than an avowed realistic confession would have been. Its meaning is not stated directly, of course, and vision and imagination are necessary for its understanding; yet "the misty mid-region of Auber" is certainly not less a part of reality than, let us say, the "circulating library" or the "County Scientific Society" of a modern, or than the turbines that one of our writers finds "close to the heart of life."

All of which means that the moderns are perfectly justified in their dogma that literature should be a revelation of life. But it should be a full and not a partial revelation; it should not confine itself to the Seen and the Known, but should embrace such life-portrayals as Shelley makes in the spiritual wanderings of an *Alastor* or as Ibsen presents in the fantasy of a *Peer Gynt.*

Closely related to the view that literature should depict life, is the narrower dogma that it should be representative of the life of a particular country. It is singular that in these modern days, when a new world order is tending to blot out international boundaries and scientific innovations have brought remote countries close together, we should be more careful than ever before about the erection of literary barriers, and should be anxious that the writers of each nation

Dogmas:
1) Classes
2) Progress
3) Revelation of life
4) Represent life of a definite country

Critories - Ordrer

corral themselves behind a fence of their own erection.

"Let us Americans write that which is distinctively American!" we cry, as though this motto were an ideal that might bear us to unimagined heights. Yet why distinctively American? And why should British writing be distinctively British, or Scandinavian distinctively Scandinavian? Does not this present an intolerable standard of national egotism? Is it not a parallel to that chauvinism which would make our fleets the largest on earth, our armies the most powerful? Or, in the narrower sense, is it not provincialism of the most shortsighted type? Is it not a denial of all claims to universality, an effort to demonstrate the superiority of our own particular product, an enrollment in a sort of religion of locality? If we Americans plead for characteristically American literature, is it not because we wish to emphasize our composite personality as opposed to the composite personality of Great Britain or France? Is it not really that we desire to make literature subservient to the tribal spirit, and that—perhaps feeling that our past accomplishments are not all they might have been—we are laboring under an inferiority complex?

The fault, it seems to me, is one of emphasis—again the old habit of mistaking the lesser for the greater. For what is the characteristic of all the finest literature?—that it is representative of a particular country, or that it represents an individual and through an individual depicts all men? To this question there

can be but one answer: it is much more essential that
a writer be true to himself than that he be true to his
locality, and by being true to himself he is far more
likely to be true to all humanity.

For, in many cases, the conditions found in any particular region are merely exceptional, and their delinea-
tion, no matter how skillful, can meet with no wide
appeal in space or time. It is only when those conditions are universal that they can give rise to enduring
literature, and when they are universal the regional
characteristics are likely to be merely superficial.
True distinctiveness in literature must arise from that
which is distinctive within the writer, must arise from
emotions, thoughts and imaginings which are but manifestations of the everlasting spirit of man; and though
they may be tempered and swayed by physical sur-
roundings, the environment at best is but a stimulus
or tool molding that which is superior to environment,
and the sense of locality cannot prevail without degrad-
ing and limiting the product.

It is so obvious as to be almost a platitude that the
greatest literature is never of a country or of an era
but rather of all countries and of all time. Shelley's
Adonais and Tennyson's *In Memoriam,* for example,
are regarded as English poems—but would their appeal
be any less had they been sung by a Russian on the
steppes of Siberia or by an Arab on the Syrian plains?
The songs of Burns, likewise, are considered typically
Scottish—yet if we overlook the outer garment of the
Scotch dialect, might they not have been sung by

Italian lover or Spanish troubadour, by Persian romantic, or lyricist of China or Ceylon?

And these illustrations are not exceptional; they are merely representative. Indeed, if one were to make a catalogue of the world's greatest literature, one would find that most of it belongs to that category for the reason that the local basis has not been made so conspicuous as to obscure the appeal to the mind and imagination of the ages.

This is not to say, of course, that there is no value in that literature which depicts the life of a particular country or community. But it is to say that there can be no general or lasting value unless the life of the region is glorified by some flash of world-wide interest, unless some facet of the universal be discovered amid the limitations of the local. And this means that the element of locality must necessarily be relegated to a secondary position, and that the emphasis must be placed upon the underlying resemblance of the setting to other settings rather than upon the underlying difference.

Whittier's *Snowbound*—to take a well known illustration—presents a definitely localized background, and is, therefore, to be regarded as rooted in the American soil. Yet might not the theme of domestic life, the theme of family striving and love and loss, have been unraveled with equal effect if the characters had been snowbound in Norway, Finland or Alaska, or even if they had dwelt in such snowless regions as Central Africa or the South Seas?

And so once more we find that the modern dogma is to be endorsed—although once more we discover that the scale of values is slightly confused.   The best literature may indeed be representative of a particular country—but that literature which is not representative of all countries is in the last analysis literature of a very low grade.

CHAPTER X

PRACTICAL FACTORS AIDING THE REVOLUTION

IN an earlier chapter we noted the fact that the literary revolution has not been entirely a natural growth, but has been aided by certain factors which may be termed artificial, since they have been deliberately planned and stimulated. And while we paused to indicate the nature of one or two of these artificial agencies, we did not deal with any of them in detail, nor did we attempt to show their extent, variety or influence. Yet it will be impossible to understand the literary revolution, and in particular its more extreme developments, without some knowledge of these subsidiary forces. Therefore, it may repay us to linger over them a while, although in essence they bear no more relation to the making of literature than the lightning bolt bears to the steeple it chances to blast.

In the popular conception of literature, such secondary phenomena play no part whatever. It is generally imagined that the literary domain is a sort of Utopian democracy, wherein justice rules unimpeded and fair play is the central luminary, wherein all applicants are equal before the court of criticism and the rights of all are decided on a basis of merit only. Although prejudice, inequality and corruption are characteristic of all things human in social or political fields, it is the popular notion that a benign impartiality reigns in literary spheres, and that, by some miraculous and unexplained process, ability will always be recognized and achievement be rewarded, so that the only criterion of literary success is inherent worth. The history of literature, of course, does not bear this out—ample evidence to the contrary is offered by the posthumous fame of Herman Melville and Samuel Butler and the belated recognition of W. H. Hudson, J. Henri Fabre, Keats, Shelley and others—but none the less the average reader remains secure in the conviction that works of merit are invariably stamped "Meritorious" and worthless works plainly marked "Worthless." Nothing, however, could be further from the facts, as a moment's consideration should serve to convince one.

Let us, for the sake of illustration, follow the career of a literary work from the moment of its birth; and let us assume that it is the novel of a new and unknown writer, but that none the less it has been written capably and with originality.

Having been brought forth in travail as the result of months or possibly even years of effort, it is sent or carried personally by the author to the offices of a large publishing house, where it is left perhaps in the charge of the office girl, perhaps in the care of an editorial subordinate. Being but one of hundreds of manuscripts submitted unsolicited by hopeful unknowns, it is in danger of receiving but a casual glance and then being hastened back to the author by express collect; but let us suppose that it is more fortunate and that, its merit being suspected, it is sent out successively to various professional readers, all of whom, in spite of a hasty perusal, return a favorable verdict, declaring that, from a literary standpoint, the book leaves little to be desired.

Is the novel forthwith accepted and published? Possibly—and possibly not. And a negative decision is quite as likely as an affirmative; indeed, it is far more likely, for the reason that the report on the literary qualities of the book is of secondary importance—the fact of major interest is the report on its *commercial* qualities. Not whether the novel will be a contribution to literature, but whether it will be a contribution to the publishers' exchequer, will be the vital consideration—and since a publisher can never know positively just what will constitute a contribution to his exchequer, he will hesitate long before deciding to take a risk on the promising unknown; his sheer conservatism and the sheer power of inertia will make him prone to gamble on the safe side— which will mean that the novelist, after a delay of a month or six weeks, will probably have the chance to submit his manuscript elsewhere.

But he will at least have one fruit of his efforts— a letter courteously expressing the publisher's "thanks" and "regrets." However, since some publishers will go out of their way to tantalize, he will perhaps be

told that "the material has been found both interesting and well written, but would not justify publication on the commercial side"; or he may read that
"None of us feels that the book has much chance of
a commercial success, but we want you to be sure that
we all realize that you have put some excellent work
into it"; or he may even be assured that "I think we
all feel the fine imaginative quality of this story, as
well as the excellent writing you have put into the
telling of it. However, when it comes down to the
question of salability, we do not believe that we could
make the book commercially successful."

And the above quotations are not merely examples
I have imagined. They are all copied word for word
from letters lent me by the actual recipients—and in
each case the sender was a long established and reputable New York publishing house.

Nor are these by any means exceptional. Other
examples might be furnished almost *ad infinitum*. Indeed, the vast majority of publishing houses seem to
feel the necessity to "come down" to the question of
salability—and the head of one prominent and successful firm has frankly informed me that he deals in
books as he might deal in hardware or furniture, and
that if he can sell the goods he will handle them regardless of their quality, but that if he cannot sell
them he will not be burdened with them no matter
what their intrinsic merit.

Now let us return to our aspiring young novelist.
By the time that he has submitted his manuscript to

six or eight publishers and received five or six letters informing him that it possesses all the virtues except that supreme virtue of marketability, his original enthusiasm will probably be considerably dimmed. But let us suppose that he is of a persistent frame of mind, and that moreover he is obsessed by an unfortunate and irresistible urge to express himself in writing, and incidentally to express himself as his own personality dictates—and not in accordance with any arbitrary conventions. Not profiting from his first experience, he will perhaps undertake the gruelling labors of writing a second novel; and, with that lack of practical sense which seems often to be the characteristic of genius, he may put forth no effort to make his book "commercial," but may attempt to write with imagination, beauty and literary style, and may even show the poor judgment to select a theme requiring an unhappy ending.

Of course, his fate will be preordained—and he will suffer for his lack of commercial instinct by accumulating a few more letters commending him upon his "interesting and well written" but unpublishable book. And if he is so courageous as to attempt a third book the outcome will be the same—while after undertaking a fourth or a fifth he will be in a mood for suicide or murder. Yet all the while he will be reading with an ironic smile the mouthings of critics who bemoan our lack of a distinctive literature; and perhaps, in order to earn a stray dollar or two to still the importunities of his landlady, he will be reviewing scores of those stereotyped but commercial novels which issue like mushrooms from our press and like mushrooms disappear to be heard of no more.

And what wonder if in the end, driven perhaps by desperation or by the need of providing for a wife or family, he should also "come down" to writing salable fiction? To be sure, he would not make the descent without a bitter ordeal of renunciation; he would feel, perhaps, as if he were prostituting his very soul; but having done his best and found that best not sufficiently commercial, what choice would be left except to do his worst, and end his career as a specialist in standardized adventure or detective stories or as contributor of serials to "Spicy Romances" or "Scandalous Tales"?

But unfortunate as would be the plight of our young novelist, it would be almost rosy beside that of his even more uncommercial cousin, the poet. While the fiction writer may at least cherish the hope of ultimate acceptance and recognition, the poet need entertain no such illusion. At least, he need entertain no such illusion unless he be gifted with an ample bank account —for it is a curious paradox that, while bank accounts and poetry naturally occupy different universes, yet those universes must merge before the poetry can cross the border-line of the obscure. It may be that an occasional publishing house will accept the full responsibility for the work of a talented but unknown young poet; but certainly such altruistic firms are entirely too rare; and since it is generally conceded that "poetry does not pay," the usual course is to permit the poet to pay instead. Of course, the poet may not be able to pay, since rhymsters are not invariably men of wealth; but in that case it is only fair that he should suffer the penalty of poverty.

But the commercial shortcomings of poetry are never so obvious as in the case of those works that from the literary point of view may be the most valuable of all—long narratives in verse. Truly, these are no longer epic days! Most publishers, although not all, will at least deign to glance into manuscripts of short lyrics; but many will tell one outright that they do not care even to look at long poems, for the reason that there is no sale for such commodities. And so, no matter how meritorious one's offering, one need not expect so much as a hearing! Dante appearing at the doors of a great modern publishing house with his *Divine Comedy,* Keats with his *Endymion,* or Shelley with his *Prometheus Unbound,* would be turned away with the statement that his work did not warrant even a reading, since obviously it was too long to be salable!

Is it surprising, then, if we find few modern *Endymions* or *Prometheus Unbounds* in print? Is it surprising if our poets turn in discouragement to the shorter magazine lyrics or even to magazine prose? Of course, if the author happens to be able to write a check that will bridge the gulf between non-marketability and publication . . . but the best poets would not necessarily be the ones that could furnish such

checks. And so, if we find that beautiful and imaginative poetry tends to be shoved aside by that coarser
and antic variety which passes the cap for the pennies
and nickels, we should not blame the poets entirely
but should give some thought to those without whom
poetry cannot appear before the public.

By this I do not mean to imply that the publishers
are to be charged with the whole responsibility—I
believe, indeed, that the fault is partly theirs, but that
in part it is ascribable to circumstances beyond their
control, to circumstances inherent in the very fabric
of civilization, to the materialistic and commercialistic
spirit that dominates modern life, to the waxing reverence for that great deity, Millions of Dollars, and to
the increasingly stringent competition which such worship implies. Our modern capitalistic system, which
seeks to standardize all things, has of course converted
books into mere articles of commerce, and has placed
printed poems and plays in the same category as stocks
and bonds; and therefore a publisher, in order to be
successful, must treat books to some extent as he would
treat stocks and bonds; while if his attitude were that
of an artist or an idealist he would no doubt be
threatened with bankruptcy.

All this I will readily acknowledge—and yet it appears to me that the great publishing houses are more
thoroughly commercialized than necessity warrants.
As the most influential of all literary judges, the
arbiters upon whom the public depends absolutely for

a continuous supply of good literature, they owe a
duty which cannot be measured in mere dollars and
cents, and for the shirking of which only their own
threatened extinction can be accepted as excuse.   Then
why, when a reputable and wealthy house is offered
a manuscript which it admits to be valuable from a
literary point of view, need it reject the book on the
ground that it is not valuable from the point of view
of salesmanship?   Are corporate dividends so su-
premely important even in the domain of art?   Must
meritorious poems, novels and plays be left vainly calling at the gate merely in order that a few executives
and stockholders may pay a higher income tax?   Publishing houses in general like to have it believed that
they are trying to put forth the best literature at their
disposal; certainly, their advertisements would indicate
that the masterpieces each year are legion—and are
they then so cowardly, so prone to flying under false
colors, that the only test which really concerns them
is that of commercialism?

One might even be inclined to forgive them were
they swayed by an intelligent commercialism.   The
sad truth, however, would seem to be that the commercialism which dominates them is as shortsighted
as it is crass; it is built upon an unadventurous conservatism, upon a plodding fidelity to habit, upon a
limitation of mental horizon that restricts their methods
to those of the machine.   For upon what basis do
these publishing business men decide what is com-

mercial? Has it never happened that they have grossly erred, and that one publisher, more daring that his fellows, has achieved huge sales from books repeatedly pronounced unsalable? If there be any method at all in their choice, beyond that favorite method of sheer guesswork, it implies the consistent elimination of all that is different, the measuring of all literary works by the pattern of that which has been known to succeed—and the consequent imputation that no other pattern can be known to succeed. The result is that the stereotyped—particularly among novels—is readily accepted, while the individual and the original is rejected as unmarketable. And so we have each year a re-issue of the same stale romances, the same crude adventure tales, the same hackneyed mystery novels in which some one is invariably killed in the first or second chapter and the villain is invariably detected in the twenty-ninth; while works in which the author has expressed himself distinctively are branded, "Excellent, but unwanted."

In all this, I believe, our publishers are not only committing a literary crime but making a grave commercial mistake. It may be, as they assume, that there is a considerable portion of the public which desires only the willy-nilly, "milk-and-water" literature; but there is also reason for suspecting that there is a fair-sized audience which would enjoy better provender, and which is merely alienated by the coarse fare now being offered. I have met persons, intelligent persons, persons well read in the literature of yesterday, who confess that they rarely turn to modern books for the reason that they find most such books tasteless and dull—and would not our publishers do well to address themselves to readers of this class? The enthusiastic welcome occasionally accorded to books of the better type would indicate that the better type of readers are not a mere handful but a veritable army—but they are a misjudged and unappreciated army; they have been neglected in order that the rabble might be fed, and have had to content themselves with dry crusts and stale meat although their palates crave ambrosia.

But let us forget the publishers for a while, and follow once more the career of our energetic young novelist. Let us suppose that he does not succumb to poverty and convention, as we have imagined; let us presume that he is gifted with a rare obstinacy, an unusual tenacity of purpose, and that he perseveres in the face of all discouragement and reaps the reward that perseverance is fabled to win. By the time that he has submitted his fifth or sixth manuscript he will possibly be smiled upon by the laws of chance; and some publishing firm, more reckless or more perspicacious than the others, may invest in what the critics will term his "first novel."

Will the pathway to fame and fortune now be open? Surely the merits of our young writer entitle him to recognition—but, unfortunately, there are still some obstacles to his success. When at last his book has been published and he begins to scan the literary columns for critical comments, he may not find himself accorded that enthusiastic applause he expects. Indeed, it may be some time before he receives even a casual notice. And when, after some weeks, the reviews begin to accumulate, they will be as likely to fill him with fury as with satisfaction; for most of them will probably be brief, and their brevity will be matched by their shallowness.

The author may find, in fact, that many of his reviewers have set out to review themselves rather than the book. One will be graciously patronizing; one will provide a list of all the recent volumes the critic has chanced to set eyes upon; one will be so consciously clever as to be palpably dull; one will make some random comments upon the book in such a vein as to prove the reviewer's total unfamiliarity with it—and the earnest and intelligent reviews will be noticeably in the minority.

The most depressing fact of all, however, will be that the earlier reviews will tend to set the tone for the later; and if the book has chanced to find space shortly after publication in a journal of wide distribution, the author may learn to his disgust that the first reviewing medium has provided the pattern for its smaller contemporaries. In fact, he may have reason to suspect that some of the papers do their criticizing by the method of the scissors and paste-pot, for either they will present a crude paraphrase of what some previous writer has said, or else they will be so frank in their admiration as to offer a word-for-word reprint—of course, without the formality of giving credit. And while our author might have some mild chance of being acclaimed, the probability is that his book would be obscured amid the multitude, would be accepted as little better than an average specimen of the year's output—and his royalties might be insufficient to keep him alive for a month.

But if he himself had had any experience in reviewing, he would surmise the reason for the cold reception accorded his work. He would know that all the great reviewing offices receive a constant flood of books, which they cannot and do not attempt to sift with any care; he would realize that well known names are always greeted with respectful attention but that names less well known have to take their chance, so that the book might either be dismissed with a casual glance, or be handed unlooked-at to a reviewer with the arbitrary injunction, "Four hundred words, please! And have it in by Friday!" And if Friday happened to be but two days off and this particular book were but one of many, there might be some gaps in the thoroughness with which the reviewer did his work.

But the author, in reflecting upon the inadequate and incompetent treatment of his book, would understand that he had little reason to expect anything better under our present system. Reviewers, he would remember, are ordinarily selected without wisdom or discrimination; no thoroughgoing inquiry is made into the merits of any applicant, and even after the candidate has been accepted, little effort is put forth to determine his particular preferences and capabilities. Our author might recall how, in the course of his own experience, he had been required by one paper to review fiction exclusively, while another would entrust him only with works of a philosophical or sociological nature, and a third would hand him indiscriminately anything that happened to be on the shelves, from treatises on biology to disquisitions on the art of lawn tennis or of cooking. And under such circumstances, he would reflect, a book must be fortunate indeed to find the proper reviewer.

He would realize, furthermore, that reviewing is subject to commercial influences akin to those which dominate so much of modern publishing. Or, to be precise, it is subject to the competition of commercial influences, for in itself it is the least commercialized of pursuits—since there are no reviewers' unions, and a living wage has never yet been accorded to the members of this most humble profession. Not only are the rates of payment low, but the time of waiting for that payment is often long, and sometimes becomes protracted into an indefinite futurity, when a paper contracts for more reviews than it can publish and some become too "stale" to print—with the result, in most cases, that the reviewer can whistle for his compensation.

And is it any wonder if, under such conditions, many potential reviewers of ability are driven from the field, while those that remain are in large part those compelled to eke out a meager existence by any means at their disposal, and in large part those forced to turn out reviews mechanically and in quantity as a sort of professional routine?

But if present-day methods of reviewing be so inadequate, how does it happen that some books, and even books of merit, do occasionally win critical applause? How does it happen that some comparatively young writers have found their way with ease to the peaks of recognition, and that apparently the road is often made smooth for the exceptional and the original book?

Leaving out of account the fact that, by sheer good fortune, a meritorious work may chance to fall on propitious soil, there are several artificial agencies through which books both worthy and worthless may be shoved into the limelight without having to undergo any of the uncertainties of competition or any of the more stringent tests of merit. As we have already remarked, there exist such things as literary cliques and dictatorships; and these, by exercising an influence akin to that of political gangs and party machines, are able to enforce their will and their policies, to advance their favorites, to crush their opponents, and to promulgate laws and ordinances which the majority must accept.

It is to be doubted whether the power of a Tammany in its most autocratic days was ever much more overweening than that of the literary Lords That Be.

Seated not behind mahogany desks on swivel chairs, but perched resolutely in front of typewriters in office and private studio, these Cæsars of the World of Books rule with an authority all the more complete in that their swords of sovereignty are unseen. As leading warriors and agents of the Revolution, they have acquired a tremendous prestige; they have taken full credit for those modern developments which the tides of the century have made inevitable whether with their aid or without. But they have encouraged the tendencies of the times to an unnatural degree, have accentuated their apparent importance and decried all opposition as treason; and by their arbitrary mandates they have set the fashion, established the precedent, and founded the court wherein all literary aspirants and offenders are tried and sentenced according to a code in whose making they had no share.

But who may they be, these literary dictators that rule with such iron power? They form no unified and easily definable group, and their citadels of authority are widely scattered; but their usual strongholds are the great cities. Some of them are to be found among the writers of magazine articles and of books; some of them occasionally wield the reviewer's pen; some are occupants of influential editorial chairs, and some at times show a leaning toward the lecture platform. Yet, whatever their differences (and their differences are wide, since one will be an autocrat of the novel, another of poetry, a third of the short story) there is one quality that they all have in common: they are the unofficial but recognized proponents of law, and beside their law there can be none other; they have decreed that literature shall be reformed, and that we have outgrown tradition—hence literature has been reformed, and tradition troubles us no longer.

And in pursuance of their principles they have issued a code of Commandments—Commandments that must be rigidly obeyed. Not the least important among them is that which demands respect for Visibility, Surface Values, and Things Easy to Understand; while others enjoin reverence for objects of great physical strength and size and for the high god Millions of Dollars, and compel abandonment of those false deities, Imagination and Beauty.

Let him who would violate these Commandments do so at his peril! The wrath of the mighty will descend upon his head; the lightnings and thunders of literary damnation will blast him; he will be consigned to an Inferno of critical contempt. About his ears will din that dreadful and accusing word, cliché, or that still more terrible indictment, "Mid-Victorian!"; he will be humiliated by comparison to Tennyson, Longfellow, or any of the vast company of the fallen; he will be derided as foggy-minded, out-of-date, and childishly unenlightened. And from the judgment of "Guilty in the first degree!" there will be no appeal. It will not matter that the accused has never subscribed to the principles he is charged with violating; it will not even matter that he has no chance to speak in self-defense. The verdict of "Literary decapitation!" will issue inexorably from the lips of the Higher Powers—and fortunate indeed will he be if he lives to lift his head another day!

The dictators, in other words, have inaugurated what amounts to an Artistic Inquisition—and the watchword of that Inquisition is intolerance, and its methods are those of the torture chamber. All who venture to dissent—and are there not still a few so foolhardy?—are conducted before the august inquisitorial bar, and are given the choice of conformity or martyrdom. Some, not unnaturally, choose to conform (since what pleasure is there in being martyred without being glorified?); but the High Chief Executioner of the new régime has not yet found his services superfluous, and it is still his pleasant duty to guillotine more than an occasional foe of the dictatorship.

But how happens it that the dictators have risen to such influence? The answer can be supplied in a single word, for they themselves would, of course, be impotent were it not for the organizations through whom and for whom they work. These, which, for lack of a more appropriate designation, we may term cliques, are in reality little more nor less than unofficial mutual aid societies. Membership in such associations, to be sure, is strictly limited, and no one joins except by invitation; but the functions of these great fellowships are delightfully informal, and no direct record is made either of the activities undertaken or of the persons involved. Moreover, everything is done in a spirit of fair play, for one has only to be a member in order to receive the utmost consideration; and one can continue to be a member so long as one has regard for that most equitable of all principles, "I help you, you help me!" This is the maxim which these organizations especially honor in their critical and editorial departments, and in particular in the department of advertising and propaganda; and, as a result, they have been able to bring their members to a prominence out of all proportion to their attainments, thereby demonstrating anew the truth of that old statement, "In union there is strength." True, some ignorant and prejudiced persons may question the benefits conferred by such secret societies, and may even insinuate that they constitute a literary aristocracy, a nobility of the self-chosen; but, certainly, there is no ground for such imputations; and the success and therefore the justification of the coöperative groups is demonstrated by the power they have conferred upon their leaders, the dictators.

So important are these literary fraternities and sororities that merit is no longer the ladder by means of which the more knowing literary aspirants climb to success. Since these are days of organized effort, they prefer to identify themselves with a group; and since they realize that influence is more efficacious than worth, they will spare no effort to make influence come their way, and will prove their sincerity by performing prodigies of egotism, and on occasion will even go so far—as one or two of our younger versifiers have recently done—as to write articles praising their own sonnets or critical volumes ranking themselves among the leading poets of the land.

Needless to say, such gallant self-confidence will be rewarded; a man who displays transcendent talents for self-advertising will be valued in this age of advertisement; the doors of the cliques will swing wide to welcome him, and in consequence he will be favored with that publicity which is balm and honey to his soul; while his more timid although possibly more meritorious fellow will suffer the penalty of a foolhardy modesty and will be enveloped in an obscurity proportionate to his contempt for the clique methods.

I do not mean to indicate, of course, that all this is characteristic of our age alone. No doubt previous eras have occasionally witnessed an unashamed self-seeking and the unscrupulous self-advancement of minor factions. Yet the conditions of contemporary life, and in particular the materialistic spirit of the great cities, have made the soil peculiarly favorable for cliques and dictatorships, and have offered especial opportunities for those who perhaps "love not art the less" but who certainly love their own interests more.

But the parading or repression of our authors regardless of inherent qualities, has not been the only result of such dictatorships and cliques. As I have already suggested, they have lent the literary revolution a new and unnatural impetus. For it happens that most of those who have launched themselves into power are friends of the revolution, so that the revolutionary policies are constantly advocated by them and their henchmen, while their opponents, not being organized, can of course not expect to make themselves heard. And therefore we find that the rebels appear far more numerous and basically far more strong than they really are,—their power is due not so much to their numbers as to their control of the agencies of publicity. And since a silent foe is an impotent one, their effective enemies are few indeed—although actually their enemies may be legion among those whose opinions find voice through no great medium of circulation.

Certainly, there would seem to be a great host of readers who, if not precisely hostile, are at least dazed and bewildered. "What do I know of criticism?" asks the average man when a judgment is handed down from Parnassus. "Who am I to dispute with those on the heights?" And so he takes a literary decision very much as he would take a prescription from his physician—it is something that is no doubt reliable since it comes from an expert source, though just wherein its wisdom consists he cannot pretend to say.

Since almost all the means of public discussion are controlled by agents of the literary revolution, normally conservative currents have been diverted into radical channels, and the revolt has gained a power out of all proportion to the social forces that motivated it. The commercialism of magazines and publishing houses,

the inadequacy of criticism and reviewing, the dom-
ineering hold of dictatorships and cliques—these are
the influences that have transformed literature more
than the embattled and turbulent conditions of the age
could ever have done unaided. Yet at the same time
the victory has been in large measure an illusion; the
agencies predominant today will probably be scarcely
visible to the future historian, and accordingly they
are responsible for whole varieties and species of books
which the future historian may never have a chance to
inspect.

CHAPTER XI

CONCLUSION

THE reader who has followed us to this point should now be able to trace a relationship between the various subjects we have discussed. He should recognize the phases of the literary revolution as the manifestations of a single but highly complex phenomenon; he should understand that that phenomenon has numerous interconnected causes and interconnected effects; and he should realize that it has not been exclusively a natural growth, but has been stimulated to a large extent by certain artificial or practical factors.

Specifically, he should perceive that there has been a correspondence between the revolution in poetic form and in prose style, and in the spirit of poetry and prose; that there is a kinship between the schools of Literal and of Psychological realism which have grown predominant and which are driving imagination and beauty from the literary field; that both those schools owe their particular character to the disturbed and blustering social forces of the day and to the nervous

haste of urban life; and that the innovators, both in
form and in substance, have been subject to the
influence of an arbitrary commercialism, of neg-
ligent critical tactics, and of literary dictators and
cliques.

But whether or not the reader has agreed with my
description of the various agencies and effects of the
literary revolt, he must have recognized that my point
of view has never been that of a member of the party
of rebellion, and that I have been inclined to look with
suspicion and concern at many of the recent developments. In short, I have been tempted to believe that
literary currents have been moving in damaging and
even dangerous directions; that much that was best
in the past has been obscured by much that is worst in
the present; that literary standards have been confused
and debased, and that the scale of values has been
lowered in the very attempt to raise it; that psychological abnormalities have stepped in where mere sanity
would never dare to tread, and that the door has been
opened to a host of eccentrics while better balanced individuals have been debarred. And I have perhaps
indicated my suspicion that, despite a great ferment
of productivity, the actual quality of our literature has
suffered through the revolution, that the inferior has
been acclaimed while the superior has been overlooked,
and that many potentially good works have been weakened if not vitiated by subservience to the new tendencies at the same time as much worthless material

has been offered to the public under the misnomer of literature.

In all this —as the reader may have divined from our foregoing discussion—there is a singular irony. While the radicals have accomplished a vast transformation in our literature, they have been curiously ill advised in the nature of their revolt—they have been moving in the wrong direction, and have inaugurated changes of precisely the opposite kind from those which the life of the times demands.

For, in this jangling, materialistic age, what need have we to be reminded of the materialism and the noise of existence?—what need to have our disagreeable everyday experiences preserved and reproduced through the medium of art? It is as if a railroad engineer were to seek relaxation amid a chorus of locomotive whistles, or as if a financier were to look for diversion amid the latest stock reports. Surely, there is enough dirt and dust in modern life without finding the squalid spread throughout our literature!—Surely, our modern cities are sufficiently ugly without having their ugliness matched by the cities of fiction!—Surely, we can encounter sufficient of the selfish and the soulless in the world without having it dealt out in concentrated doses in our books!

It is not that we would flinch in confronting life or in understanding it (for do not most of us realize how bleak and unattractive it can be?); it is not that we would escape from the realities of the earth to the cloudly glamour of some remote empyrean; it is that we would have all things presented in their true colors and proportions, that we would not overemphasize the obvious nor relegate the less material phases of existence to an undeserved obscurity. In our daily lives there are certain facts which are insisted upon unduly; we have time to see only surfaces, time to feel only surfaces; we are so energetic in our pursuit of concrete values that we have little chance even to communicate with ourselves; and we are surrounded by such ugliness that we forget the possibility of beauty, and are steeped so much in the matter-of-fact that imagination would impress us as akin to absurdity. And because our lives tend thus to be led on an inferior plane, should we take precautions never to lift ourselves to a superior? —should we see that literature descend to meet our experience rather than that our experience rise to meet literature?—should we demand that our creative output be limited in accordance with our own limitations, and that the scope of art be as narrow as the range of our own vision?

To me it seems worse than absurd that, merely because there are phases of life which are closed to the ordinary experience, those phases should be forbidden territory to literature as well. In an age when the normal environment is unsightly and uninspiring, let literature be more inspiring and more beautiful than ever!— In an age that makes most of us mere plodders amid prosaic and insipid facts, let the wings of a poetic fancy be unfolded to their widest! Not by illustrating the deficiencies of life, but by counteracting them, literature can perform its greatest service; and the most valuable prose and poetry will be that which is well rounded and full blown, that which lays emphasis upon those intangible qualities we are tending to neglect— qualities that lie scarcely noted in the still and silent recesses of the ultimate soul of man.

But is it probable that we will have such a literature? The answer depends, of course, upon the permanency of the tendencies initiated by the revolution. If the modern movement remains dominant, we must expect the literature of visible values rather than that which sounds the labyrinthine caverns of the beautiful and the intangible. Whether the modern movement will indeed remain dominant is, of course, more than mere criticism can undertake to say; but if I would hazard a generalization by way of prophecy, I would suggest that the movement, while approaching its final stages, is at present too fluid and changeable to assume an aspect of permanency, so that a reaction from its more extreme phases is not unlikely to reverse the pendulum and inaugurate literature of quite a different type.

Yet it is inconceivable that a development so varied and wide-reaching should pass and leave no trace. Though the revolution should indeed flutter out and be forgotten, it will probably bequeath certain tendencies to be embodied in the literature of a later age—tendencies which will represent the distilled essence of all that is best in the aims and methods of the present innovators.

But we need not confine ourselves to such vague prognostications—there are grounds for arriving at somewhat more definite conclusions. Not only the social causes of the revolution, but the practical factors aiding it, furnish us with important clues. To begin with, we are fairly safe in believing that so long as modern life remains unchanged, modern literature will continue to move in its present channels; so long as men are subject to a continual mental tug and strain, there will be something strained and nervous about literature; so long as the minds of our people are occupied mainly with material things, material things will continue to hold a literary seat of honor. If the personalities of our writers and readers are so obsessed with the clamor of cities that they are not susceptible to the faint, indefinable vibrations of beauty, then beauty will be excluded as effectively as a violin melody might be excluded by a triphammer. If our imaginations are overcast by a fog that blots out the stars and limits our vision to five-story rows of brick, then imaginative things are likely to have the permanency of snow-flurries in a tropical July. In appearance, of course, there may be tremendous changes; there may be a continual experimentation in form, and a constant withdrawing of veils; there may be a more daring realism, and a more determined attempt to photograph naked facts—but in spirit we can expect no fundamental transformation until there is a corresponding transformation in the spirit of life; until our overrushed and mechanical civilization no longer clouds the spirit of man and no longer frustrates the deeper manifestations of personality.

But while we should have to begin with economic reform in order to modify the social basis of present-day literature, the difficulty is not so profound when we turn to the practical factors aiding the revolution. Since these have been in large measure created and stimulated by artificial means, they must necessarily be subject to conquest by artificial means; and since their effect on the revolution has been wide-reaching and their power to magnify existing influences has been enormous, their elimination would mean the end of some of the most deadly scourges afflicting present-day literature. Once limit the ravages of commercialism, sponsor a finer critical spirit and terminate the rule of the cliques and dictators—and literature would be on the way to exercising anew the freedom which it once enjoyed and which the apostles of a false liberty have denied: the freedom of open fields and the woods, of polar oceans and sunset clouds, of moonlight and stars and of those pathless solitudes which are the land of dreams, and those uncharted airy realms where the hopes and fancies and ecstasies and desires of man go ranging unseen.

But how can so exalted an end be consummated? How can literature win back its lost independence? I do not say that we can even begin to accomplish all that we contemplate, nor do I predict that in practice we shall accomplish anything at all; but I do believe that there is much that we may do, and that the ultimate power resides with those who have long been disenfranchised in the republic of letters, and who, did they but know it, might proclaim their rights and cast the decisive ballot.

For it is not the writer, not the editor, not the professional critic, that in the last analysis is literature's supreme arbiter; it is the discerning lover of books, the man whose approbation or disfavor may mean the final prominence or obscurity of any literary work. And it is this man who has been most neglected. The literary dictators, as we have already indicated, have been applauding that brand of literature which conforms to their particular taste, regardless of the taste of the masses of intelligent readers; and the masses thus far have been singularly patient, and have done their best to adjust themselves to what they try to regard as superior standards of appreciation. But they need not persist in their efforts at adjustment. Once they rise and demand recognition, once they rise and insist that literature be no longer frivolous and eccentric, but that its aims be serious and its standards of art consistent—and they will find that they have been attacking castles of paper. All opposition will vanish from before them like a mist—they will discover that their patronage is essential even to the Lords That Be, and that the threatened withdrawal of their patronage will be an argument before which Commercialism itself will bow in respect. Thus far they have been despised or disregarded, and at the same time they have been voiceless and meek, accepting humbly that which was doled out to them; but let them once refuse to accept, let them require a more satisfying literature or none at all—and they will find that, genie-like, the Lords That Be will be ready to offer them that which they ask.

Certainly, the mere lover of books has some right to be considered even in these days of the Dictator-ship. And, certainly, his potential power is as light-ning to blast the commercial machines and the cliques. But will that power be utilized? Unfortunately, it is not possible to answer definitely; we can only say that the future holds intriguing possibilities, and that a re-volt of the Literary Proletariat would be quite as in-teresting a development as the present revolution itself.

Even in the absence of such a revolt, however, litera-ture does not seem likely to continue indefinitely on its present track. For some time it may proceed along an almost unswerving path, changing in superficials rather than in substance; then, possibly after a period of years, there will be some unforeseen social develop-ment, some revolution in thought or in life, some sudden shifting of the tides of civilization—and the effects will tremble and reverberate to the very heart of literature, stimulating it or shocking it into fresh activity, altering its direction and transforming its tenor, giving it a new color, a new earnestness, a new energy, and so serving not only as the beginning of an epoch but as the end of one of those cycles which mark the course of all revolutions in literature and in the world of visible events.

THE END